BED RUGS

18th and Early 19th Century
Embroidered Bed Covers
Expressions of the American Spirit

Jessie Armstead Marshall

ISBN: 0-9708930-0-0
Library of Congress Control Number: 2001126143

J.A. Marshall, 52 Spring Hill Rd., Storrs, Ct. 06268-2513
Printed and bound in the United States of America for the author

Dedicated to the late
William L. Warren
whose interest and knowledge
of antiquities inspired many persons

Contents

Illustrations

Front Cover Photo

A New England bed rug located at the York Historical Society, York, Maine (Photo courtesy of York Historical Society)

Back Cover Photo

The embroidered bed rug made in 1976 by the author (Photo by Herman F. Marshall)

Acknowledgments

The author is indebted to a considerable number of persons and organizations for the material that went into the making of this volume. Responses to inquiries have been generous and useful in my search for bed rug information.

Although care has been exercised to make acknowledgment herein of every one of these persons and organizations, the author begs the indulgence of any who may inadvertently have been omitted.

First I am indebted to the late William L. Warren for his encouragement and for his gift to me of his research on bed rugs, the foundation of this book; also to the late Israel E. Liverant of Colchester, Connecticut, and Mrs. Joanna Liverant; to Mr. and Mrs. Arthur Liverant of Colchester; to my brother, the late George B. Armstead Jr. and my sister-in-law, Doris Field Armstead. Also to the Connecticut Historical Society, and the Antiquarian and Landmark Society Inc. of Connecticut.

I am also indebted to the staff at Bolton Town Hall, Bolton, Connecticut, the staff at Booth Dimock Library, Coventry, Connecticut; the Old Goal Museum, York, Maine, to Christine Stevens, curator at St. Fagan's Museum of Welsh Folk Life, St. Fagan's, Wales; Mr. and Mrs. Arthur Halpern of Renate Halpern Galleries, New York City; and to Kay Midgett Sheppard of Tennessee. I benefited from the kindness and wisdom of the late Miss Marion Frye, a former faculty member at the University of Rhode Island, and to William Mottes for technical advice.

I am grateful too, to the love and encouragement from my husband, Herman F. Marshall, without whose support this book would never have been written.

This list of persons is by no means complete, and I wish I had the names of all those who helped me in museums and libraries, and to those who encouraged my endeavors, during the research and writing of this book.

Introduction

My interest in bed rugs began in the 1960's when I became fascinated with a group of black and white bed rug photos my husband was reproducing into color slides for William L. Warren, then curator of the Connecticut Historical Society in Hartford. The variety of wonderful designs in the photos Bill had collected made a lasting impression on me. The embroidered covers contained simple motifs, but were bold and striking in their entirety. They seemed to me to be unique in the world of American needle arts.

A few years later a Connecticut antique collector asked me to repair a 1741 bed rug before it was to be placed in the 1972 bed rug show at the Wadsworth Atheneum. I took several months to study the rug and several more months to repair the damage from moths, vermin and general neglect. This project added to my interest in bed rugs and increased my appreciation of their construction.

At the bed rug show, the first show ever held exclusively featuring bed rugs; I was awestruck by the bed covers that were on display. They were portraits attesting to the inventiveness of American women of the 18th century. The rugs expressed the women's love of color and love of nature, combined with a generosity of spirit that was not allowed to blossom in the old world. They displayed in their rugs their newfound freedom. Little did they realize they were creating one of the first statements of the new world, later aptly phased by Walt Whitman as "I hear America singing..." Those great, embroidered covers sang to me that day at the museum, and it was then that I knew I had to make a bed rug.

I started my rug in 1973 using an antique hand woven blanket and many yards of my own hand spun, natural dyed yarn. Three years later I initialed and dated my finished bed rug. Upon its completion, Bill Warren said I was the first person to have made a bed rug since 1833. This is the date of the last known dated bed rug, now only a fragment, on display at the American Museum in Bath, England.

I had the pleasure of seeing my rug exhibited at the Great River Show at Wadsworth Atheneum in 1985. This show depicted three centuries of items made in the Connecticut River Valley of New England. My rug and other contemporary river valley hand made items were displayed at the Lions Gallery of the museum. Since that time I have repaired two more bed rugs, each made in the last quarter of the 18th century, one by Patience Foote of Westchester, Connecticut, and one made in the Connecticut River valley area by Lorraine Collins. I have tried to view and review as many rugs as possible, those that had been exhibited at the 1972 show, as well as those that have been found since that time.

More recently I spoke briefly and displayed my rug to those attending the June 1999 Dublin Seminar for Early American Folk Life, held in conjunction with Boston University, the American Antiquarian Society, the Society for the Preservation of New England Antiquities, and Historic Deerfield.

This book is a culmination of my notes from working with antique bed rugs and creating my own bed rug; in research, into what others wrote about bed rugs, from a time when they were considered hooked rugs, to today's informed writers with more knowledge of this type of needlework.

I, like John Taylor, the Water Poet, have written a book in praise of the needle. Needles were the paintbrushes of the women of early America and their palettes were tinted with dyes from the new world.

Taylor, a Thames waterman as well as a poet, included in his book on needlework a poem titled *The Prayse of the Needle.* I hope the thoughts expressed in this extract from his poem will also be true of my book on bed rugs.

"All these are good, and these we must allow,
And these are everywhere in practice now:
And in this Booke, there are of these some store,
With many others, never seen before.
Here Practise and Invention may be free,
And as a *Squirrel* skips from tree to tree,
So maids may (from their Mistresse, or their Mother)
Learne to leave one worke, and to learne another,
For here they may make choice of which is which,
And skip from worke to worke, from stitch to stitch,
Until in time, delightfull practice shall
(With profit) make them perfect in them all.
Thus hoping that these workes may have this guide,
To serve for ornament, and not for pride,
To cherish vertue, banish idlenesse,
For these ends, may this booke have good successe."

John Taylor (1580-1653)
The Prayse of the Needle

What is a Bed Rug?

Bed rugs are colorful expressions of the American spirit. Like so many other types of folk art, the bed rug is a wonderful example of ordinary people doing extraordinary things. The bed rug making technique was similar on both sides of the Atlantic, but the designs of the New World covers are an outstanding example of the American exuberance for life.

While the word bed rug was used both here and abroad for 200 or more years to refer to a shaggy, coarse bedspread, the American-made rug developed into a creative outlet for women colonists throughout the 18th century, and continued for several decades in the 19th century. Early Americans would have their handiwork in a prominent place in their homes, as this type of fancy bed covering graced the top the best bedstead in the best chamber, often on the first floor of their house.

The earliest known bed rugs were made in Eastern Massachusetts, and were unschooled designs placed on woolen blankets by the makers own ability, and not copied from a teacher's pattern book. They contained most of the elements of later more schooled designs, the hearts, flowers, zigzag patterns, scalloped borders, sunbursts, initials and dates, but remain fresh and delightful in their simplicity.

Over the past 70 years, antique textile authorities have tried to explain the American bed rug. Many failed in the early days to realize that these covers were embroidered, and not hooked. Two articles in *Antiques* magazine in November 1927 stated that bed rugs were hooked, and an article in *Antiques* magazine in 1934 printed double talk by stating that bed rugs were embroidered with some kind of hooking technique, occasionally using a needle. In fact, the two techniques are completely different. Hooking is made with a crochet-like tool, and looped pile running stitch embroidery is created with a needle. This stitch was the only known bed rug stitch at that time. Since then, bed rugs have been found with several other types of stitches. The editor of the magazine referred to the rugs as wool on wool covers. At that time, wool on linen bed rugs were undiscovered. Bed rugs are distinguished from other embroidered coverlets as the background material in a bed rug is completely covered with needlework.

The word rug means a "coarse coverlet, a rough woolen material, a sort of coarse frieze in common use during the 16th and 17th centuries," according to the *Oxford Unabridged Dictionary.* Continuing the description the dictionary stated a rug was a "large piece of thick woolen stuff (frequently of various colors) used as a coverlet or as a wrap in driving, railway travelling." It also referred to the word rug being used to describe wearing apparel.

In 1667, Samuel Pepys (1633-1703) recorded in his diary on July 13 "Mighty hot weather. I lying this night with only a rugg and a sheet upon me."

Samuel Johnson, author of a dictionary published in 1755, described a rug as a bed covering with similar terms as used in the unabridged dictionary. In an English gazetteer printed in 1778, the town of Lancaster, England was described as "a city famous for the manufacture of coverlets, rugs, blankets, and other sorts of bedding." A coarse, nappy woolen cloth is the description of the word, rug, American Noah Webster published in his 1835 *Dictionary of the English Language*. He also described a counterpane as a covering for a bed, and a coverlet as an upper bed cover.

Dictionaries describe the word shag as rough matted hair or wool, the nap of a long and coarse cloth, a garment, rug or mat of shaggy material. Florence Montgomery used a similar description for rug in her book, *Textiles in America*.

Among the goods transported for some of the colonists in 1629 were 50 mats, 50 rugs, 50 pair of blankets of Welsh cotton, 100 pair of sheets, 50 bed ticks, and bolsters with wool to put in them. Joseph B. Felt wrote in *Customs of New England* in 1853 that rugs were coarse, nappy coverlets for common beds used by our "primitive" families. He stated that such articles have been little known among our furniture for the last half-century and the word denoting them is seldom applied in such a sense. The word rug he stated now (1853) means floor mat.

The rug is described as a covering for a bed, and carpets as coverings for floors in *Colonial American English* by Richard M. Lederer Jr. He described the word shag as a kind of cloth with a long, coarse nap used for clothing and bedding.

A variety of names for bed covers were used in the 17th through 19th century. The most common are: coverlets, rugs, counterpanes, quilts, and the more modern terms are bedspread, puff and comforter.

The use of each type of cover was listed in Essex County, Massachusetts, in an article written by George Francis Dow. He cited that between 1635 and 1674 coverlets were mentioned 142 times, bed rugs were mentioned 157 times, and quilts four times. He further stated that description of these rugs included cotton rugs, English rugs, Irish rugs and cradle rugs.

Dow quoted from a book written by the Rev. Nathaniel Ward of Ipswich, Massachusetts, titled *Simple Cobbler of Agawam* published in 1647, "To cloathe Summer matter with Winter Rugge, would make the Reader sweat."

Upon the death of Mrs. Joanna Cummings of Salem, Massachusetts in 1644, an inventory of her possessions included a green rug among the bedding, and the 1641 inventory of John Goffe of Newbury, Massachusetts, taken in 1648 also listed a rug.

Dow makes an interesting observation by noting that quite a few bed rugs have survived into the 20th century, but none of the bedsteads, which held these shaggy covers, exist today. Early bedsteads were described as vividly as their coverings using such terms as high beds, side beds, canopy beds, half-headed, joined, cabin, corded, close, press, standing, truckle, trundle and cradle.

Careful inventories were taken of the more well to do colonists. In 1656 Mistress

Glover's household furnishings in Cambridge, Massachusetts, were listed by servants, and recorded by Thomas Danforth. The inventory included a suite of blue and a suite of green bed furnishings with rugs, and mentions other rugs as well.

Rugs in Early Probate Records

Terms used in describing bedding in early probate record inventories were almost as diverse as the inventory takers. Some terms used to describe rugs included a shag blanket, Irish and Polish rugs for beds, rugs by the yard, a sad (brown) rug, a rug eaten, probably meaning moth eaten, and a worsted 'stript' rug. Many rugs were listed by color; the most popular was blue, followed by red and green. Other descriptions were a silk rug, and a rag rug, probably not a floor rug, as the item was found among the bedding in the inventory. Other adjectives associated with rugs were striped rugs, blue and white rugs, bird's eye rugs, plain rugs, cabin rugs, cradle and thrum rugs. Thrum rugs were often made with left over yarn found at the ends of a bolt of fabric. Thrums were often left on fabric bolts to show the purchaser that he was buying the entire bolt, and not being short-changed. Also listed was a rug coverlet, which probably meant this item was found as the uppermost cover on the bed. The most important find in this research is that no description of rugs mentioned floral designs, the colorful rugs, which decorated so many colonial bedsteads. The rugs mentioned in the inventories were probably shaggy woolen bed covers, similar in weight and usefulness to their colorful counterparts, but nowhere near as artistic an item. These fancy, floral or geometric designed, home made works of art were probably given away before the maker or owner died, and therefore not listed in an inventory.

The probate estate inventory of Captain Myles Standish written Dec. 2, 1656 and exhibited at the court held at Plymouth, Massachusetts included several rugs. One rug, spelled rugg was listed with a blanket and a "coverlid", two "ruggs" were listed with a blanket and one old rug was listed with a feather bolster. The feather beds and bolsters for the most part were more highly valued than the rugs or other types of blankets. The inventories were usually taken room by room and each room's bed would be listed separately as the inventory takers proceeded through the home of the deceased. John Alden and James Cudworth signed the inventory.

Many rugs were found in the 1667-68 inventory of Edward Wharton of Salem, Massachusetts, including a light colored worsted rug, five sad colored worsted rugs, six green and blue plain rugs, a cabin rug, a coarse rug, and a red rug. Also listed in the estate were two silk rugs, 16 country rugs, and a large silk rug.

Customs and life styles of eastern Connecticut towns in the early 18th century resembled eastern Massachusetts, where most eastern Connecticut settlers originated. It can be assumed that the bed rug making technique found in early Massachusetts towns would be continued in Connecticut. The earliest known bed rugs came from the eastern Massachusetts towns of Wenham, Ipswich, and North Andover. Eastern Connecticut towns where bed rugs were made include Coventry, Colchester, Pomfret/Hampton, New London, Lebanon, Norwich, Bozrah and Canterbury.

Bed rugs were not limited to Massachusetts and Connecticut. The use of the term is found in an inventory in Kittery, Maine in 1682, describing the bedding of a canopy bed as having bedding rugs and blankets.

Merchants in Boston sold bed rugs among other household furnishings. An item from the *Boston Gazette* dated Sept. 1, 1760 listed "Scotch floor carpets, counterpins, Bed Ruggs, scarlet and crimson check for bed curtains." Another item in the Dec. 29, 1760 *Gazette* advertised rugs of green and blue worsted yarns. A rug fitting this description, a plain colored, looped-pile rug is in the collection of textiles at Winterthur Museum in Delaware.

Probate records for Connecticut in the 17th century show the use of bed rugs among the household goods. While not all wills were accompanied by a complete inventory, and though most included only the disposition of money and land, several from 1635 to 1668 did list rugs. It is not certain what kind of rug was used on the beds, but this type of cover was distinguished from blankets and coverlets.

In the inventory of Seth Grant of Hartford, Connecticut, filed on March 4, 1646, one rug was listed among other bedding. It was valued at ten shillings, and a coverlet was valued at one pound, ten shillings. The rug was either inferior to or more worn than the coverlet. One rug for a bed was listed in the June 7, 1664 inventory of the estate of William Backus of Norwich, Connecticut. Aside from his land and cattle, his clothing was valued higher than other inventoried items. Many times valuable possessions of a person would be given away before death, to avoid probate.

In a will dated April 17, 1666, Elizabeth Watts of Hartford, Connecticut gave her cousin, Daniel Hubbard, a green rug. The will of Sarah Ensign, also of Hartford, taken May 29, 1676, gave her grandchild, Sarah Rockwell, one-half dozen napkins, one pair of sheets, and the best rug. It is evident from this will that the rug was a valuable item, but it is not known whether it was imported or home made, floral or plain. An inventory of the estate of Susannah Bushnell of Hartford taken after her death in 1683 listed a feather bed, bedstead, bolster, two pillows, pillow cases, a pair of sheets, three old curtains, two old blankets and one old rug. The total value was six pounds, three shillings. Alexander Douglas died in 1688 in Hartford, and among his effects left to his daughter, Sarah, was the best bed, bolster and "my best rug." Bolsters were long pillows used on beds along with regular pillows. People enjoyed sleeping in a near sitting position.

Inventories taken in Massachusetts during the 17th and 18th century are very similar to those taken in Connecticut and New York and reflected the use of much bedding due to the number of persons in a family and to the cold winters of the northern colonies.

Furnishings of the bed chambers of one home in Roxbury, Massachusetts in 1691 contained a feather bed, bolster, two pillows and pillowbeers (pillow cases), two blankets, a coverlet, rug, painted calico curtains, valances, bedstead, mattress and cord. The cord was the rope used to tie the bed together. Also listed in the home was a parlor chamber containing a down bed, two pillows, pillowbeers, a good green worsted rug and other bedding, and in the kitchen chamber, a room above the kitchen, was a rug among other bedding. The Rev. Jose Glover's widow married Henry Dunster, president of Harvard

College in 1641. Among the furnishings of her home was a blue rug for a bed, blankets, coverlets and other rugs to 'furnish' beds. The inventory of William Clark of Salem, Massachusetts who died in 1647 listed among the bedding a green rug covering a bed and a second green rug on another bed in the same room.

In the 1660 inventory of William Paine of Boston, Massachusetts three rugs were listed in the warehouse chamber, a rug among other bedding in a little room, an old red rug in the hall chamber, and a rug and blankets in an attic chamber.

Of the 83 inventories listed in Hebron, Connecticut, probate records written from 1784 to 1796, 20 various types of rugs were listed. These records covered many inventories taken in the towns of Hebron, Bolton and Coventry. Many rugs listed had some sort of descriptive phrase and all were listed among the bedding. With this position in the inventory it is safe to assume that they were used as bedding not as floor coverings. At this period of time few persons could afford floor carpets of any kind. The bed rugs were described as white, bird's eye, pile, shag, old, and rag. The highest value placed on a rug in this group was in the inventory of the estate of Daniel Badger of Hebron, taken July 3, 1792. It was valued at one pound, six shillings, five pence, and the second most valuable bed rug belonged to Rachel White of Coventry. It was valued at 24 shillings in the Sept. 20, 1790 inventory. Bed rugs were not as plentiful as coverlets and quilts, for 128 coverlets, 84 quilts, and only 20 bed rugs were listed in this group of inventories.

Among the bedding listed in the inventory of Noah Owen of Hebron made on April 21, 1791 were two shag rugs, each valued at only two shillings, a striped rug at four shillings, and a flowered coverlet at 10 shillings. The flowered coverlet might have been an embroidered bedspread or bed rug. In the inventory of Ezekiel Jones of Hebron in 1792 an old rug of pale blue was listed among other bedding. Colonel Joel Jones of Hebron, a prosperous man, died in 1792. The inventory included six beds and fittings, three underbeds, eight coverlets, six quilts, numerous sheets and blankets, as well as a loom and fittings and three spinning wheels. One of the items described was a baize bed quilt. Baize is a heavy, woolen cloth that is well napped. Jones also had a compass worked coverlet valued at 20 shillings and an older compass embroidered coverlet along with three rag coverlets. The compass embroidery on a coverlet, discussed in a later chapter, is a pattern, resembling the compass design found on maps. It was usually applied by simple embroidery to the corners of a woolen blanket. A tape loom was also listed among Jones' effects. This small loom was used to weave a narrow strip of linen fabric, one-quarter to one-half inch wide, that was used to attach curtains to canopy beds, window curtains to rods, and to make apron and garment drawstrings. Many times the weaving of tapes was a chore given to children. From this inventory it can be assumed that some of the household members were weavers, spinners, and needle workers. In such a home a bed rug might have been made.

On July 3, 1792 the inventory of Jesse Cook of Coventry, listed among the bedding a blue (compass) rose coverlet at 18 shillings. This could have been a blue blanket embroidered with a compass rose design. He also owned a blue rug at 16 shillings, a red rug at 16 shillings, a figured coverlet at 15 shillings, and a blue and yellow coverlet at five shillings. A figured coverlet might have been an embroidered bed rug. He also owned a loom and yard goods.

Nathan Ingraham of Hebron owned several coopering tools, used by barrel and tub makers. Also listed in the 1792 inventory after his death were a curtain and tester sheet, and a dye tub, which he had probably constructed. The estate, inventoried in 1794 of Captain Ichabod Phelps of Hebron, contained tools for preparing wool for spinning, and Levi Loomis left a loom, five spinning wheels, and logwood dye along with two rag rugs among other bedding, according to the inventory taken after his death. It is evident from these inventories that a great deal of fabric was made at home.

In the inventory of Captain Samuel Robertson of Coventry dated 1794 an old rug was listed along with 13 quilts and nine coverlets. Also listed were a rather rare item in rural areas, window curtains. Robertson also owned a loom and fittings, a cider mill and blacksmith shop. He owned 95 acres on a highway, and his entire estate was valued at £400.

Another important citizen of the time, Samuel Kingsbury of Coventry, left in his estate in 1794, five beds and fittings, one underbed, seven coverlets, and four rag rugs. The rugs were presumably for beds as they were listed with other bedding. The estate also included woolen and linen bed curtains, and woolen and linen window curtains. This is another industrious family as there were two looms, a rope wheel, and a cider mill in the estate. Cider mills could be operated by water, but were often operated by a horse.

Two prominent men of the Richardson family of Coventry in the late 18th century left interesting inventories upon their deaths. The first was Amos Richardson who died in 1779. The majority of the inventory was clothing including several coats, vests, a morning gown, breeches and shirts. Among the bedding listed were linen sheets, woolen sheets, a bed quilt, two coverlets and one old rug, spelled "wrugg" which was valued at £6. The sheets were valued at £9. His bed was valued at £20. His son, Captain Amos Richardson, whose inventory was taken in 1803, showed the Captain with more possessions, more clothing and more bedding than his father had owned. The bedding did not include a bed rug but did include a rose blanket.

Families were often busy with several occupations in addition to farming, and yet many women still had time to embroider blankets and make curtains. One early inventory included an embroidered pocketbook. Fancy items such as an embroidered pocketbook, needlepoint bible cover, or embroidered shag mittens were given as gifts.

A number of the inventories listed rag rugs among the bedding, and it is impossible to tell just what this description means. Today rag rugs mean floor carpets woven with heavy string-like cotton or linen warp, with weft strips of cotton or woolen fabric inserted into the warp by the use of a large shuttle. Bed rugs fashioned on the loom using this rag rug technique were a common item in the French area of Canada, and were called catalogne. Catalogne bed covers were made with salvaged fabrics in the weft, first of wool and later of cotton, and some were a mixture of fabric and woolen yarn. They were still being made in the early 20th century, and these later rugs were most often woven with narrowly cut cotton sheeting-weight rags, which were inserted into a cotton warp. The rugs, both heavy and bulky, were used as the top covering on beds in less affluent homes. Other types of bed covers were made and used by wealthier Canadians including boutonne covers, a type of woven embroidered cover. The embroidery would have been inserted during the weaving. French Canadians also made woven coverlets as well as quilts. Canadians in the Maritime Provinces of Eastern Canada, many of Scotch-English descent, also wove bed rugs of rags and yarn, similar to their French Canadian neighbors in Quebec. They also used old fabric salvaged from blankets, sheets and clothing, as well as woolen yarns. Few wool rag bed rugs from this area survive today.

In the latter part of the 19th century the rag rug was relegated to use on the floors of homes in both the United States and Canada. This became possible when factory woven fabrics became inexpensive.

Sources of Design

The oldest type of surviving needlework in England is ecclesiastical embroidery. Domestic embroidery followed in the wake of church sponsored needlework. English needlework was the greatest source of patterns for English speaking Americans.

One of the earliest surviving pieces of needlework in England is the Bayeux Tapestry. It was made by an ecclesiastical group in Canterbury, England and depicted the Battle of Hastings, where William the Conqueror of Normandy defeated England's King Harold in 1066. The tapestry was commissioned by the Bishop of Odo, a brother of William, and was made at a nunnery in Canterbury in 1067. The tapestry was a tremendous undertaking even by today's standards. It is an embroidered work not a woven tapestry.

A close look at the designs used in the 230-foot long by 20-inch high frieze shows the extensive use of colors and a variety of motifs. As it depicts mainly battle scenes, more men than women are included in the work. Other designs include horses, dogs, mules and birds, as well as buildings, ships, boats, trees, vines and written words. All these elements were found in later English and American embroideries. Many of the tapestry's designs compare in artistry to Psalm books printed between 966 and 1066. Some historians believe English women made the tapestry, because the more subtle designs show items of which Norman French women would have had no knowledge. David J. Bernstein discusses the English origin theory in *The Mystery of the Bayeux Tapestry*.

In Elizabethan times in England, women did very little with all wool embroidery, perhaps because so many silk and precious metallic threads were available to the wealthy, and wool was relegated to the poorer class citizen's needlework, little of which has survived. Inspiration for the embroideries made by the upper class would come from emblem books, illustrated Bibles, a few British and European pattern books, and from the flower and fauna of the English countryside.

Gillyflowers were a very popular design in the 17th century for embroidery. This name was applied to many carnation-like flowers with a scent of cloves. Also popular in needlework were 'woodbynes' (woodbines) or climbing plants, such as ivy and honeysuckle, and 'trafels' (trefoils) or three-leafed plants of the clover family. More than 100 pattern books were published in the 1500's in Germany, Italy, France and England. They contained floral, geometrical, pictorial, and animal motifs. Pattern books from the Continent were little used by English needle workers, because they were not readily available in England, and the continental patterns were not popular in England.

Several books with embroidery patterns that were available to 18th and 19th century needle workers, especially in England, include *La Clef des Chames* by Jacques LeMoyne, a French painter. The book was published in 1586. Also, *A Schole-house for the Needle* by Richard Shorleyker published in 1624, and *The Needle's Excellency* by J. Boler. The last edition of this book was published in 1640.

Some English pattern books were copies of European works. A few English pattern books contained original artwork. It is these original books that most appealed to English needleworkers, and many early domestic embroideries can be traced to these few books. The two books most widely used were works by J. LeMoyne and R. Shorleyker. It is believed that Shorleyker copied some material but that the leaves, flowers and animals were his own designs. LeMoyne copied some designs but it is thought that his floral motifs were his own.

Most of the bed rugs that are extant were made in New England. However, the sources of design probably came from outside this area. Traffic with Europe, especially England, was constant, only interrupted by war. Even during times of conflict trade managed to elude enemy ships, and American privateersmen brought back captured goods, which were sold at seaports all along the Atlantic coast.

Textiles and pottery from Europe and the Orient were decorated with designs, which could be adapted to needlework. Imported volumes, including the Bible and other books, illustrated with fancy designs, imported hatboxes covered with decorated paper, and imported document boxes lined with decorated papers were other sources of needlework designs.

American needle workers sought out English and French designs, which were used with less detail and stitched with surface filling stitches making lighter, more airy work than European items. There would be fewer flowers, vines and other motifs on each article, and less complicated stitches were employed in the New World. Silver and gold threads were used less frequently than abroad. A distinguishing feature of New England embroiderers was the use of large flowers in both crewel and bed rug making designs. Floral patterns on bed rugs were much larger than on crewel-embroidered articles of the same period.

Some designs were popular both here and in England, especially the brilliantly colored flame stitch pattern, sometimes referred to as a Florentine stitch. The English used this zigzag, banding design embroidered with silks, for bedding. The design also can be found on pottery and marbleized paper. T' ₋ flame stitch has continued to be used on upholstery fabrics throughout the 19th and 20th centuries.

Americans mainly used bright colored woolen yarns to create the flame stitch pattern. An example of this pattern is found in several bed rugs. One woman used a variety of shades of blue to make the pattern, and Mary Avery used this design in her rug made in 1722. The motif was also used in a rug owned by the Daughters of the American Revolution, Faith Trumbull Chapter of Norwich, Connecticut. The rug, made about 1741, is of knotted pile created while the rug was being woven.

Other popular English motifs found in bed rugs are a large central pattern outlined at the bed edge, the all-over floral design, the shell design, and a two-handled vase design.

Hearts and flowers rising out of a vase were popular in both bed rugs and in samplers in the 18th century. The use of names, initials and dates were used on many bed rugs but never to the extent of the inscriptions found on samplers. This is probably due to the technique of making the bed rug with its coarse wool and large embroidery compared to the fine silks and worsted threads used when making samplers.

The major sources of designs for embroidery in the New World were ideas brought from their former homes in Europe, imports of goods such as wallpaper, household items, fabrics, finished embroidery, and the surroundings of the colonists, the flowers and fauna of their new homeland.

Simplicity in American embroidery was the major difference between European and American needlework, and the most popular design in the New World was flowers. Floral designs take many forms and shapes, but all are easily recognized from the poorest to the most artistic rendition. Leaves, vines, trees, birds, animals, fruits, border designs, shell shapes, loops, geometric shapes, baskets, bowls, and vases were other popular motifs in bed rugs and other embroidered textiles.

There are no known books with patterns specifically for bed rugs. Bed rugs were inspirations of the makers and they used designs from other needlework, especially samplers. Some were copies of other bed rugs. Similarity between bed rugs is common. For example the Colchester, Connecticut area rugs used intricate darning stitches and patterns as well as similar color schemes.

While there were few pattern books published in America, patterns were collected here by needle workers and teachers. In addition to pattern books, individual patterns were printed abroad, and were for sale in larger cities in Europe. *The Ladies Magazine*, which printed patterns, began publication in London in 1774. These items were imported to America. While most patterns published were for use on clothing, embroiderers adapted the designs for other items. Designs created for men's waistcoats and women's stomachers could, through American ingenuity, find their way onto bed rugs. The little designs would have been enlarged and simplified, then applied to the bed cover.

One of the rare American examples of embroidery designs to have survived is the book of patterns gathered by Elizabeth M. Townshend. It is an 1815 manuscript of over 190 patterns. and is now known by the title, *Early American Embroidery Designs*. Miss Townshend probably collected her patterns during the late 18th century as well and the early 19th century.

Some of the patterns in her book can be found on bed rugs, including the M's and W's design, scallops, fish scale designs, fruits, nuts, trefoil leaves, two-handled vases, tulip-style flowers. daisy-shaped flowers, and rosebuds. These designs were probably traced from the manuscript and then enlarged for use on bed rugs, bed hangings and window curtains. and used as drawn for clothing and small items such as samplers and pockets.

Bed rug designs followed a similar course of popularity to samplers. There seems to be no flowers in vases before 1742, and no hearts used before 1751. The one exception is the hearts found on the 1722 rug made by Mary Avery of Massachusetts. Inscriptions were found on embroidery pieces after 1662, and borders of naturalistic flowers did not appear until 1730.

Some American embroidered pieces were executed with English yarn on English fabric and taught by English teachers, which makes identification as a truly American made item almost impossible unless a name and town was worked into the fabric. The bed rug is the exception because of its truly American conception. Imported bed rugs were most often described as plain colored, spotted, striped or streaked. No referral to floral designs in bed rugs has been found in searches of American probate inventory records.

Early 19th century books and magazines that were devoted to women's work often included patterns and instructions for embroidery. Although they were probably published too late to be of use to the majority of bed rug makers, the information contained in them would have been passed down from mother to daughter and circulated through local girls' schools, years before the publications were available to the public. *The Lady's Book* published in 1830 in Philadelphia by L.A. Godey & Co. and *The Handbook of Needlework* by Miss Lambert first published in 1840, are two examples of 19th century needlework publications containing designs that were probably popular during the previous several decades.

Early New England Schools

The idea of girls being educated in town operated schools was discussed and recorded in many towns, but few of these towns actually provided girls an education, and those towns that did, offered much less to girls than to boys. It took nearly 200 years from the founding of the country to place girls on an equal footing with the boys. Until then the young women had to content themselves with reading and needlework skills. These needlework skills far surpass the ability of most of the female population in this country today.

The earliest reference to girls in public schools was mentioned in 1639 in Dorchester, Massachusetts. The document stated the decision of whether girls should be taught with boys was left up to the discretion of the elders. The elders consisted of seven men. No other reference was made so possibly the discussion never arose.

Hampton, New Hampshire made an agreement in 1649 with the schoolmaster, John Legat, that he should instruct children of the town, both male and female, to read, write and cast accounts. No records remain as to whether this was ever carried out.

An edict in Watertown, Massachusetts in 1650 allowed girls to be taught writing and casting accounts if they had the desire. The town of Dedham, Massachusetts discussed the education of girls as well as boys in 1652, but no record is left concerning education. Deerfield, Massachusetts agreed in 1698 to educate girls from four to six years old and boys from four to eight years old. A tax on the parents of school age children was set at £10 annually whether the children attended school or not.

Girls and boys were taught English, writing, and to cast accounts in Rehoboth, Massachusetts by Robert Dickson in 1699. It is known that few girls were sent to public schools in Northampton and Hatfield, Massachusetts before 1680. The winter term of school in Hatfield in 1700 listed four girls and 42 boys in attendance, and in 1709 16 girls and 64 boys attended school. Whately, Massachusetts claims that girls always attended school with boys and pursued the same studies.

Farmington, Connecticut voted funds for the instruction of children in reading and writing in 1687, and the next year the town stipulated that male children, who had learned their hornbook, could attend. Girls were generally not admitted to the public school in this town. Hopkins Grammar School in New Haven excluded girls in 1680. Other towns excluding girls in the late 17th century were Norwalk, Connecticut and Hadley, Massachusetts. However Meriden, Connecticut allowed girls to attend school in 1678 according to town records.

Administrators of the estate of Thomas Gridley in 1655 in Hartford, Connecticut ordered the estate to educate the sons to read and write, and the girls to read and sew well. A similar decision was made in the estate of Thomas Thompson in 1656 ordering the estate to provide education in reading and sewing for girls, and reading and writing for the boys.

One of the earliest records of building a school for girls is recorded in Hingham, Massachusetts in 1761. The town voted to erect a schoolhouse to be used as a female school. The building was to be situated near a school for boys. This same town voted in 1791 to instruct girls in reading, spelling, writing and needlework. About 1800 the town decided some of the girls, 12 years and older, might attend male schools in the winter months, and boys under nine might attend certain female schools in summer months. In Gloucester, Massachusetts, girls were taught reading, knitting and sewing according to town records for 1707.

Most schools for girls were privately run before 1800 and they taught reading, spelling, sewing, embroidery, and sampler making. Writing, arithmetic, grammar and geography were considered unnecessary for the female mind. There were exceptions to this as is recorded in Marblehead, Massachusetts in 1792, at which time the town founded an academy for girls and boys. The school was attended by both girls and boys seated in the same class on opposite sides of a large hall.

When Nathan Hale kept school in New London, Connecticut in 1774, he wrote to a friend that he held a morning school in summer between the hours of five and seven for about twenty young ladies. He received six shillings a scholar by the quarter.

There were three kinds of dame schools, the private neighborhood establishment that was held in most towns; the semi-public dame school sanctioned by the town and augmented with some public funds; and the public dame school, which finally merged with regular summer school with a woman teacher. This school eventually became the public primary school. The dame school taught the simple rudiments of reading to both sexes.

An Oxford, Massachusetts dame school teacher, Miss Betty Jermer, made figures in the sand floor of her home with a rod, to instruct the children, who wrote on birch bark with pieces of charcoal. In 1717 the first dame school teacher mentioned in Windsor, Connecticut records was Sarah Stiles, and the following year the town voted the schools were to be open in the summer until October. Early dame schools were kept in private homes, not school buildings. Spinning schools were held for poor children so they could obtain work by spinning. The pay was so low for dame school teachers that women often had to augment their income by other jobs, such as spinning, tailoring and dressmaking.

School buildings were not a priority in colonial New England. The first buildings to be built after houses were the meetinghouse, gristmill, and the pound, an enclosure for stray cattle. For example, Springfield, Massachusetts was settled in 1636 and was recognized by the General Court of the colony in 1641. They built a meetinghouse in 1644, and a school in 1679.

Before a town built a school, classes were held in private homes or other town buildings, such as town halls, meetinghouses, parish houses, almshouses, shops, and even barns. When a school was built it was often quite small. In Springfield, Massachusetts a school 22 by 18 feet was built in 1679, containing five windows and chimney. Thomas J. Stebbins Jr. was paid £14 for his efforts. This would be about $622 in today's money. In the city of Boston in 1704 John Barnet was paid £l00 to build a 25 by 40 foot school with eight windows. He was given the material from the old school house as well. His pay by today's scale would be over $4,000.

Dr. Thomas B. Downer, town physician of Stowe, Vermont held school in his home after his arrival in 1800 with his wife and two young children. This was the first school in the town that had been founded in 1794. Records mention that a second schoolhouse was erected as early as 1803 after the first log school building had burned.

In an advertisement in the *Connecticut Courant* on Dec. 1, 1812, a school committee comprised of three men, Levi Wells, Asa Willey and Wareham Foster were looking for a builder to construct a school in the town of Ellington, Connecticut. The advertisement read as follows: "Any person who wishes to contract to build a School House, the walls either of brick or wood, and to furnish all or part of the materials, is requested to call on the subscribers and receive a plan of said proposed house, and make known his terms."

In that same issue of the *Courant*, a grammar school in Canton, Connecticut advertised that they had room for 12 scholars to be taught grammar, geography, arithmetic and penmanship. In the North West (school) District of Hartford the school committee was advertising to hire a schoolmaster.

Another advertisement advised readers that the Winstead Academy in Winchester, Connecticut would open on Dec. 9. The teacher, Curtis Warner would instruct "the languages preparatory to entrance into college and such other branches of literature as are usually attended to in similar schools."

When schools advertised for students, the school committee usually meant they were only holding classes for boys unless they specifically stated girls in the advertisement.

Schools for Young Women

While no 18th century newspaper advertisements can be found in Boston, New York or Hartford, Connecticut that specifically stated they taught bed rug making, many school teachers did advertise plain and fancy stitching classes along with academics, music, dancing and other 'genteel' arts. As only elementary embroidery stitches were needed for bed rug making, most young women would learn simple embroidery stitches and plain sewing at an early age, either at home or at school. The most popular hand stitched articles made by young women were samplers, mourning pictures, coats of arms, embroidered clothing items, and pocketbooks. These articles were often mentioned in newspaper advertisements for girl's schools. The embroidery patterns from these items could be transposed to other articles including bed rugs. While most students were taught the art of sampler making as a beginning project, this important item served the student as a guide to stitches and patterns for other embroidery projects.

Anne MacVicar Grant's memoirs were written in the years previous to the American Revolution. Miss Grant tells of a child being brought into the household of an uncle in Albany, New York in 1709, and how fortunate the youngster was to be able to reside in this household where she could receive an education. She recalls that Colonel Schuyler looked upon his seven-year-old niece with much favor. Although he had sons and daughters, he realized that this niece, Cataline, was eager to learn and he provided an education for her. It was difficult to procure instruction for girls in the inland areas such as Albany, and female education was conducted on a limited scale. Girls learned needlework from their mothers and other female members of the household. They were taught to read in Dutch, by reading the Bible and religious tracts. English was not often spoken, and few learned to read English. Lower class citizens had little or no instruction, especially girls.

Young Cataline left her uncle's home after the death of her father. Cataline married her cousin, Philip Schuyler in 1719 when she was 18 years old. She lived near the Indians, was friendly with them and encouraged them in their crafts, including basket making. The Indians used embroidery techniques to decorate their baskets by stitching patterns into the vessels with sinews of deerskin, and employed European designs to accomplish this decoration. They also used some woolen worsted yarns to make sashes, according to the author, who knew Cataline Schuyler when she was an elderly woman.

Sarah Anne Emery wrote in her book *Reminiscences of a Nonagenarian*, that several schools were open in her hometown of Newburyport, Massachusetts, during her childhood. These schools taught young women sampler making, pocketbook instruction, the embroidery and construction of mourning pieces, and coats of arms as well as basic stitching, knitting, plain sewing, drawing and water color painting. In describing her own home, Miss Emery mentions only quilts and coverlets when referring to bed furnishings. Born in 1787, she wrote the book in the 1870's, and died in 1879.

Anna Green Winslow wrote in her diary, while she was attending sewing school in Boston in 1771, that she had made her aunt a 'decorative and practical' pincushion. She also mentioned studying sewing, needlework, and writing in school, and knitting at home. In 1770, when she was 12 years old, Anna Winslow came from Nova Scotia to attend school in Boston. She died in 1779.

One of the most famous schools established for women in the 18th century, was Miss Pierce's School of Litchfield, Connecticut. It opened in 1792 and was advertised as an untried experiment. Previously the education of young ladies, with a few exceptions, had been taught by their mothers or was neglected. Miss Pierce's School ran until 1833.

Another young lady, Eliza Bowne, wrote a letter home on February 13, 1798 in which she said she was studying embroidery and geography at school and wanted permission to study music. She was a student at Miss Rawson's school in Boston. In her book, which contained the above letter, Miss Bowne described a tour of a Bethlehem, Pennsylvania sewing school, where 120 students attended. She wrote of the beautiful embroidery done by the students at this school, mentioned seeing embroidered pocketbooks, pin balls (pin cushions), toilette cushions and artificial flowers. The Pennsylvania school also taught music and other branches of education according to a booklet that the author obtained during her tour.

Newspapers throughout the colonies contained many advertisements for schools for ladies and gentlemen. In a 1774 edition of the *New York Gazette and Weekly Mercury*, Sarah Long from London advertised a school for young ladies at which reading was taught. Mrs. Susannah Condy advertised an embroidery school near the Old North Meetinghouse, Boston, in 1743. She had patterns from London but drawn by her at a cheaper rate than the English drawings. She also sold embroidery materials and needles. Mrs. Condy's daughter, Elizabeth Russel, advertised patterns for sale in her shop near a Boston drawbridge, in 1747. These were probably her late mother's drawings.

In 1755 Elizabeth Hinche of Long Lane, Boston, living in the house of Mr. Jonathan Clark, advertised she was an embroiderer who was proficient at plain sewing, Irish stitch, tent stitch, sampler work, and other sorts of needlework. Jean Day taught embroidery at Mrs. Cutler's boarding house in Williams Court, Corn Hill, Boston, according to an ad in the *Boston Gazette* in 1757, and Eleanor M'Glvaine taught embroidery in an establishment near the governor's residence in Boston in 1758.

While none of the ads stated that they taught young women to make bed rugs or any other type of embroidered bed furnishing, simple embroidery stitches were taught at most all schools, and these were the stitches employed in making bed rugs and other embroidered bed covers.

One of the best-known schools for young women was the Balch School in Providence, Rhode Island. The students at that school were known to be so proficient in needlework, that upon completion of their instruction at the establishment, they often became teachers. Mary Balch's mother, Sarah Rogers Balch was probably the teacher, as the designs deteriorate after the mother's death in 1811. The senior Mrs. Balch probably started teaching after the death of her husband in 1776. There is no evidence that bed rug making was taught at this school but it is certain the skills needed to make a bed rug was one of the elementary courses taught at the school. A country school was established in the small community of Andover, Connecticut in the spring of 1808. An advertisement for young women was printed that year in the *Connecticut Courant*. The headline stated "Education, Miss Mary F. Morse." The ad continued "Respectfully acquaints the puvblis that a school commenced in Andover (Connecticut) in the center of said Society, on the 13th of June for the instruction of young ladies, in the following branches…"

She offered classes in reading, geography, English grammar and composition. She also taught plain sewing, marking, muslin work and embroidery along with drawing, landscape, flower, and figure painting in watercolors and "phillagree with various other kinds of fancy work."

The ad continued, "Miss Morse, happy in devoting her time to the arduous, though pleasing task of female education, and hoping, by the strictest attention to the manners, and morals, of her pupils, to merit the approbation of the public; now solicits its generous patronage." She made it known that application to the school could be made at the residence of the Rev. R. Ryler, and that the boarding of students was available on 'reasonable' terms. Between the classes of plain sewing and embroidery, marking and drawing, a young woman would have all the skills needed to stitch a bed rug or any other embroidered bed cover. The other skills needed for bed rug making, weaving, spinning and dyeing were most often taught at home.

A school for young ladies was advertised in the *Connecticut Courant* on May 25, 1813. The Goshen, Connecticut school was operated by Miss Mary North. Classes in reading, writing, grammar, geography, history, rhetoric, composition, painting and embroidery were taught.

A school in Northampton, Massachusetts advertised in the *Connecticut Courant* on May 20, 1817. Miss Clarke was the teacher and her classes included instruction in music on the pianoforte, French and drawing in addition to the "ordinary branches of education."

A lengthy advertisement was placed in the *Connecticut Courant* Dec. 7, 1813 that announced a new boarding school for young ladies would open in January. Mrs. Value wrote that she would teach classes in plain sewing, needlework on muslin and embroidery in addition to reading, writing, as .onomy, arithmetic, English grammar, geography, composition, drawing and painting. See Appendix for the complete advertisement.

While the education of women in the early days of this country seems sparse to us now, the instruction received by the majority of women, from their family and the little schooling available, enabled young women to survive the rigors of life in the 18th and early 19th century. Most young men never received more than a rudimentary education in the same period, as only a few were able to afford a college education.

Embroidery Stitches Used in Bed Rugs

Most bed rug makers used the most common embroidery stitch, the running stitch, but they added a loop to each stitch to create raised pile embroidery, that gave the rugs their shaggy appearance. The thickness of the strands of yarn and the height of the loops create the texture of the rug, and variety could also be accomplished by leaving the loops cut or uncut.

Pattern darning is darning used as embroidery, worked in parallel rows using straight stitches of various lengths to form a design on the surface of the background material. The best darning needlework effects are created when the background material is evenly woven with easily counted threads. This type of embroidery is derived from the utilitarian method of mending or reinforcing a fabric. A number of parallel rows of running stitches worked evenly to resemble weaving become darning stitches.

Pattern darning, unlike mending darning, does not always have as even a stitch. Mending tends to go under the fabric as much as over the fabric. Pattern darning appears most often on the surface only dipping under two or three threads, and over five or more threads of the background fabric. The pattern is formed by use of the background fabric, and the background fabric is much more important when using this stitch than in a rug made with the running stitch. Pattern darning takes a more accomplished embroiderer, and takes more time to fashion.

Darning samplers taught at girls' schools here and abroad were a reference work for the student to use not only for mending but also for decorating items in her post-school days. The diaper design, a diamond-shaped design, was a very popular darning stitch, along with the herringbone, striped, and checked patterns. The several rugs made by women who lived in the Colchester, Connecticut, area and the Lorraine Collins rug are examples of darning stitch embroidery.

Stem stitches were used by one bed rug maker. The stem stitch is similar to the crewel stitch but is made with the needle going into the fabric at a greater angle than in the crewel stitch.

Some rugs were made with a knotted stitch, while still being woven, and sometimes the knots were made after the fabric was taken from the loom. The stitch was made by inserting the needle into the fabric from above, leaving one half-inch to one-inch length of yarn on the surface of the foundation. Proceed by going under two weft threads, then bring the needle back up to the surface and enter the foundation fabric again at the original point of entry. Then repeat this by bringing the needle back to the surface and cut off the yarn. This creates a knotted tuft of yarn that looks like a double loop. This stitch is repeated across the fabric in horizontal rows, following the colors for the pattern and background designs.

Diagrams of Stitches Used in Bed Rugs

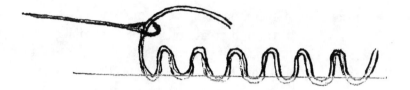

Looped-Pile Running Stitch

Stem or Whip Stitch

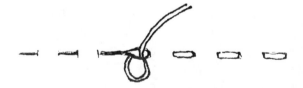

Darning Stitch

Pattern Darning Stitch

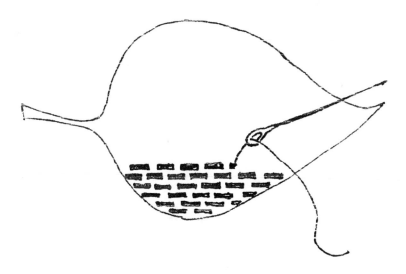

Pattern darning embroidery is worked in parallel rows using various lengths of stitches, to form a design on the surface of the background material. This style bed rug has a smooth surface. A diamond-shaped pattern, called the diaper design was very popular, as were the herringbone, striped and checked patterns. The design to be worked with pattern darning was usually outlined with a running stitch.

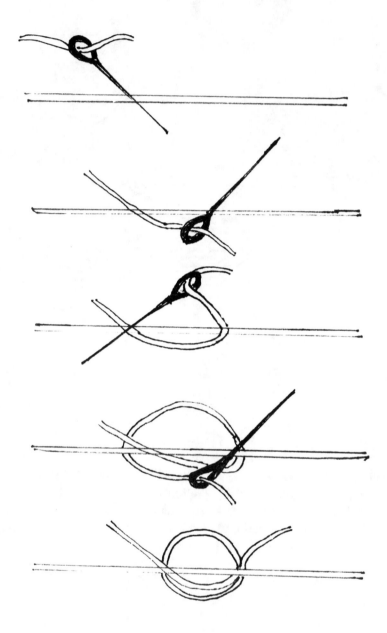

The double-stitched pile used to create a bed rug now located in New Brunswick, Canada, is made by inserting the needle under two weft threads, coming back to the surface, entering again at the original point, and then returning to the surface. The tufts are made in horizontal rows.

Bed Rug Makers

Who would have made or owned a bed rug? Bed rug makers would not have been found among the poorer families, who had time only for the essentials of life: food, shelter and warmth. Bed rug makers and owners probably would not have been among the more wealthy early Americans either, as they would have emulated their counterparts in England, and purchased imported silk embroideries. The wealthy Americans' possessions would have included fancy bed furnishings of the latest imported silks and woolens with window curtains to match, mirrors decorated with silk embroidery, fancy firescreens, wall plaques featuring coats of arms, and embroidered document and sewing boxes.

The poor lived in very small homes, some not larger than 18 by 24 feet for as many as eight people. There would have been no room for a loom, perhaps only a spinning wheel, and there would be little spare time to embroider even small items. Plain sewing of clothing and mending for the family would be the only needlework. It was recorded that a Massachusetts pauper lived in a one-story house, 16 by 12 feet with a thatched roof. Many of the poor had chimneys built of sticks and mud. Thatched roofs and stick chimneys were soon outlawed as too hazardous in early New England.

The parlors in many homes were often used as a bedroom. In the inventory of the John Dillingham estate in 1634, records show that the parlor of his two-room home contained two bedsteads. The bedding was valued higher than the bedsteads. Coverlets were mentioned in the inventory but no bed rugs. The other room in his home was a kitchen, and was referred to as the hall. This room did not contain a bed.

Bed rug makers would have come from middle class families who mainly resided in rural areas where imported bedding was not readily obtainable. There are exceptions to this as in the case of bed rug maker, Rebekah Harris who lived in New London, Connecticut, a prosperous seaport town in the mid-18th century.

By that time many Americans were members of this middle class and could afford some of the luxuries in their homes that heretofore had been available only to the wealthy. Many of those refinements were more often made rather than purchased by the middle class Americans. Among those homemade items would have been bed rugs, samplers, embroidered blankets, calamanco quilts, and clothing embellished with embroidery.

One of the earliest bed rugs, the Thorn rug, dated 1724 was pictured in the June 1930 issue of the magazine *Antiques* and the editor commented on its unusual pattern in that it deviated from the normal embroidery designs of that period. Despite the fact that he believed these covers were 'hooked' he still thought of them as important documents of the period. Articles such as this helped in the preservation of bed rugs by bringing them to the attention of collectors and historians.

Many of the bed rug makers are discussed in the following pages.

The Hale Family Bed Rugs

Several members of the Hale family of Coventry, Connecticut made bed rugs. A rug dated 1776 was made by Rebekah Harris of New London. Rebekah, born April 16, 1749, married Joseph Hale, third son of Deacon Richard and Elizabeth (Strong) Hale of Coventry, and a brother of Nathan Hale, the patriot. The marriage took place Oct. 21, 1778 and the couple settled in Coventry. They appeared to have lived on a farm in South Coventry. Joseph also ran a sawmill. Rebekah was the daughter of Judge Joseph Harris of New London.

Rebekah's rug was made before her marriage when she was living in New London. She fashioned the bed cover with a running stitch with cut and uncut pile on a wool plain weave foundation comprised of several sections. Two shades of blue, two shades of green, a greenish tan color, and several russet shades were used for the pattern stitching, and the background was stitched with a natural undyed yarn. The rug measures 91 inches in length and 89 inches in width. The design features a central bouquet rising out of a multicolored bowl and is surrounded by a bold vine that begins at the central foot of the cover and wanders up each side of the rug. This design is referred to as a branching floral bush surrounded by a vine-like floral border. This is one of the two fashionable designs of the last half of the 18th century, vying in popularity with the tree of life designs. The rug is located at Smithsonian Institution.

Rebekah's husband, Joseph Hale, served in many capacities during the Revolutionary War; including answering the Lexington Alarm, serving with the militia in New York, and as a lieutenant with Knowlton's Rangers. He was probably at the Battle of Harlem Heights in September 1776. He was captured by the British in November 1776 after being wounded but was exchanged for a British prisoner. He was back in active service the next year. Joseph died April 30, 1784. The family thought he never really recovered from the effects of the war on his constitution. At the time of his death he left four daughters, Elizabeth 5, Rebecca 3, Polly 2, and Sally, a newborn who died two months later. After her husband's death, Rebekah took her little girls to live with John and Sally Hale at Hale Homestead on what is now South Street in Coventry.

It is believed that Joseph's widow occupied the northwest (parlor) chamber at Hale Homestead. When the widow Rebekah remarried, it appears that her daughter Rebecca (Becky) remained with the childless John and Sally Hale at the Homestead. Rebekah (Harris) Hale was married for the second time about 1787 to Thomas Abell of Franklin, Connecticut. She died March 1814 at the age of 65 and Thomas Abell died Dec. 8, 1824 at the age of 82.

Bed rug maker Sally Kate (Hale) Clapp, oldest child of Enoch and Octavia (Throop) Hale was born in 1782 in Coventry. She was the niece of Nathan Hale, the patriot, and sister of Nathan Hale, the editor of the Boston Daily Advertiser. She was raised in Westhampton, Massachusetts and in 1800 married Elisha Bascom Clapp (1779-1860) of Westhampton.

Her rug was made on a dark brown woolen plain weave foundation of three widths and measured 102 inches long and 91 inches wide. The embroidery was made with the running stitch with cut pile and features a serpentine feather design reaching from the base of the spread to the top from which large flowers and leaves in shades of olive greens, light browns, tans and faded yellow were stitched. Her initials S C and the date 1806 were placed in the central top of the cover. This rug is located at the Governor Jonathan Trumbull House in Lebanon, Connecticut, owned by the Connecticut Daughters of the American Revolution.

Philena McCall (1783-1822), daughter of Ozias and Elizabeth (Williams) McCall of Lebanon, Connecticut made a bed rug that might have a possible Hale family connection. She married Deacon Eliphet Abell, also of Lebanon in 1806. The rug remained in the Abell family until 1970 and is now at the Wadsworth Atheneum in Hartford, Connecticut. The McCall family and the Hale family were related through the marriage of Sarah Clapp, daughter of Sally (Hale) Clapp and Elisha Bascom Clapp, who married her cousin, Hobart McCall, son of Henry and Melissa (Hale) McCall of Lebanon in 1853.

Philena McCall's rug is one of the best examples of design and color in bed rugs. It was dated 1802 and initialed P M. It features a two-handled vase in the central portion of the rug from which five large flowers emanate. Around the bottom and sides of the rug are undulating feathered vines and flowers of all shapes and sizes. The embroidery is done by the running stitch with cut pile in shades of rust red and olive green on an undyed background. The fringe is made with two shades of olive green.

Another rug with an intriguing history is attributed to a Melissa Hale. It is initialed M H and dated 1804. In a 1913 article in *House Beautiful* magazine, the rug was attributed to Melissa Hale, niece of Nathan Hale. No verification of her relationship to Nathan Hale could be found. The rug pattern starts with a vine and floral design at the foot of the rug and winds around each side to the head of the rug. A floral bouquet is set at the center of the rug. No color description was given in the article that was illustrated with a black and white photograph. Unfortunately the location of this rug is unknown.

The Foote Family Bed Rugs

Among the many women who created bed rugs, were several women, who lived in the Colchester, Connecticut, area. They made rugs that were quite similar, and were executed with a great deal of embroidery skill.

The bed rug initialed E F was probably made between 1760 and 1780. It might have been made by Elizabeth (Kimberly) Foote, the wife of Israel Foote. Daughter of Ruth (Hale) Kimberly and Thomas Kimberly Esq. of Glastonbury, Connecticut, she was born on June 30, 1715 and married to Israel Foote on Dec. 28, 1748. She died Jan. 6, 1798. Israel Foote, born Oct. 16, 1713, was the son of Nathaniel and Ann (Clark) Foote. He died Aug 17, 1788. However there is no proof that she was the bed rug maker. Another possible maker of this rug is Elizabeth Foote, the oldest daughter of Elizabeth (Kimberly) Foote and Israel Foote of Colchester. She was born on May 29, 1750 and married the Rev. David Huntington on Nov. 5, 1778. Another possible maker of this rug is Esther Foote who married Caleb Gates of East Haddam on Oct. 17, 1775. Another woman, Eunice Foote, who was born on March 13, 1759, could also have made the rug. These women were grandchildren of Nathaniel Foote of Colchester. The rug is now owned by Connecticut Historical Society.

The second daughter of Elizabeth and Israel Foote, Mary Foote, was born April 3, 1752. It is believed that this is the Mary Foote that made a bed rug in 1778, even though she spelled her last name as Foot rather than Foote on the rug. This rug is at Winterthur Museum, Wilmington, Delaware. Mary was married to Nathaniel Otis, son of John and Prudence (Taintor) Otis. The Otis family was a close neighbor of the Foote family.

Elizabeth and Abigail Foote, daughters of Israel and Elizabeth (Kimberly) Foote each wrote interesting diaries in 1775-76. Abigail's diary contained many short entries for about half the days in each month. One entry for Saturday, June 1775 was "I helped Mol make a Bonnet for mother and a bonnet for Ellen...." Mol was Molly or Mary Foote. Many entries in both diaries mentioned daily activities including weaving, carding, spinning, warping the loom, quilting, making candle wicks, picking goose feathers, making quilt batting, knitting and sewing many types of articles including dresses, shirts and trousers. All these activities were in addition to housework, candle making, cheese making, berrying, attending weddings, funerals, church meetings, town meetings and visiting with friends. A great many of the activities were done with other family members and friends. An entry on Wednesday, April 12, 1776 that shows her awareness of the Revolutionary War stated "I got out a piece of cloth for a loose gown for mother and for myself and went to the widow Well's in the afternoon and there was a general Muster at Mr. Otis'." She made an interesting entry on Monday, Aug. 26 "I carded and went to carry some tansy to Esq. Foote to be stilled and rid old pipsy and got as wet as a drown'd rat." Tansy was used to cure several ailments.

Elizabeth Foote's diary is similar to her sister's in style and activities. Both women were very busy. She wrote entries for almost every day from January through October 1775. Elizabeth mentions more knitting projects than Abigail and often wrote about going to school in the early entries of the diary. Evidently Abigail was not attending school at the time she was writing her diary. One of the more revealing entries in Elizabeth's diary was made on Tuesday, April 18, 1775 "I rose before the sun and made apple pies and dumplins for breakfast..." and on Friday, April 21, 1775 she wrote: "In the morning we heard they had begun to fight at Boston." Another entry shows her expertise in assorted activities as on May 13 she carded tow and helped her sister make a broom of Guinea wheat straw. One entry suggests that she had knowledge of needlework design as she wrote on Wednesday, Sept. 1775 "I did house work and drew a quilt border for Mrs. Blush." On Tuesday, Oct. 24 she writes, "I lay a bed till sun an hour high. I got up and carded a little while and then writ journal for 2 weeks back and Alice went home sick after she had spun 4 knots. Procrastination is surely the thief of time." It is easy to see why her journal was not written daily with the amount of activities crowded into a day. Neither sister mentioned making a bed rug or any other embroidery project but with their expertise in sewing and all their other accomplishments, bed rug making would have been easily done by either of these young women.

A bed rug similar to the Colchester women's rugs is now at Historic Deerfield Museum in Deerfield, Massachusetts. It is unsigned and undated, but it is so much like the Colchester rugs that it is probably from the same area in Connecticut.

The flowers in these rugs include several types of carnations, many-petaled daisies in several forms and many fanciful flowers. Interspersed with the flowers are a variety of leaves, from simple ovate forms to multi-lobed designs with central veins. The leaves and flowers are tied together by wandering vines twisting around each large floral motif, and anchor at the foot of the rug in a large leafy design. Some of the rugs also have realistic acorns stitched in a close-set pattern.

Each flower and leaf is diversified from the others by the variety of count-thread embroidery done with the darning stitch. The variety of stitches results in a checkerboard effect, a diamond pattern, zigzag diagonal line, straight line and many other diverse geometrical patterns. Even flowers, which have a similar shape, become completely different in appearance due to the complexity of the embroidery. In one bed rug more than 20 different darning stitch patterns were used.

Samplers made to show a student's proficiency in the darning stitch technique were taught to young women at many schools in this country including the Westtown School in Pennsylvania and the Balch School in Rhode Island.

A rug with similar embroidery, but a different color scheme, is the Lorraine Collins bed rug, which is discussed in a later chapter.

The Colchester rugs are an important group of rugs because of their well-designed patterns and intricate embroidery. These women outlined each section of a motif with the outline stitch and filled the area with darning stitches. Flat running stitches were used for the background. The background fabric is completely filled in as in all bed rugs, but this type of embroidery does not create the shaggy loop-pile effect of the other bed rugs. One more striking aspect of these rugs is their sparing use of color. Each used several shades of blue with brown or black for the design and an off-white yarn for the background color. The Colchester rugs were more artistic in design and execution, presented a more formal appearance than all the other bed rugs. To create these rugs, the women used a large central bouquet, which in some cases was held together by a double-handled vase. This was surrounded with large floral patterns tied to each other by wandering vines, that began at the foot of the bed cover. This central block lay on the top of the bed, and the floral and vine design ran around the fall of the bed cover.

Another Colchester area bed rug was made by Patience Foote, daughter of Nathaniel and Patience (Skinner) Foote of Westchester Society in the town of Colchester. She was born on Feb. 1, 1783 and died June 19, 1859. Patience married William Brainerd of Westchester Society on Oct. 31, 1797. Her husband, a farmer, was appointed captain of the home militia and served a number of years as surveyor and collector for the town. He was the son of William and Lucy (Day) Brainerd of Westchester The rug, made about 1799, is initialed PF and was found in an Eastern Massachusetts home of a Brainerd family descendant circa 1989. It is privately owned.

The Patience Foote rug is different from the other Colchester area rugs. It is not made with the count thread darning stitch and does not have a similar layout and design to the other Colchester area rugs but she did use similar shades of colors. Patience made her rug with the loop pile running stitch and designed her rug on the popular tree of life design with three vine-like trees proceeding up the rug from the foot to the top. Each tree was filled with many types of floral motifs and leaves. Her flower patterns are similar to many other bed rugs but the overall pattern does not closely resemble any of the other known bed rugs. An undulating scalloped-edged border was stitched on the two sides and the foot of the rug. She applied her initials boldly at the head of the bed cover. In some respects it is like the Mary (Hinkley) West cover made in 1763 in its tree of life design and the loop pile running stitch embroidery with uncut pile. However the colors used in the two rugs are quite different. Mary (Hinkley) West's rug is discussed in a later chapter.

A woman with the surname of Foote made a different type of bed cover. It was a white trapunto quilt and was created by Lucy (Foote) Bradford in 1816 for her dowry. This could be the Lucy Foote who was married to Merrit Bradford of Canterbury, Connecticut on Feb. 28, 1821. They lived in Newburgh, N.Y. where he was a teacher at the Academy. He died in 1846. Lucy was the daughter of Capt. Aaron Foote of Colchester and Mary (Isham) Foote, who were married in 1774. Lucy's mother died in 1804, and her father died in 1824 at the age of 80.

The Hannah Baldwin Rug

The Hannah Baldwin bed rug is dated 1741 and initialed H.B. A small paper at one time attached to the back of the rug stated "Baldwin" "senior". This paper probably was written to distinguish the maker of the rug from other women with initials H.B. who were members of the Baldwin Family. The bed rug also contained a linen patch upon which the initials H.B. were embroidered in cross-stitch. The sheet from which the patch was taken could have been made by Hannah (Knowlton) Baldwin, the senior, or made by her daughter or by one of several women in the family with the same initials.

The probable bed rug maker, Hannah (Knowlton) Baldwin was the daughter of Thomas Knowlton and Hannah (Green) Knowlton and was living in Canterbury, Connecticut in 1741, at the time the bed rug was made.

Thomas Knowlton, the father of Hannah (Knowlton) Baldwin, died on Feb. 28, 1717 in Ipswich, Massachusetts. Her mother, Hannah (Green) Knowlton, the daughter of William and Hannah (Carter) Green of Devonshire, England, died in Norwich, Connecticut on Oct. 24, 1708. Hannah (Knowlton) Baldwin's parents spent time in both Ipswich and Norwich, two areas where bed rugs were known to have been made.

Hannah (Knowlton) Baldwin married Benjamin Baldwin, son of Benjamin and Hannah Baldwin. It is not unusual to have two families with similar given names running in each generation as the name Hannah does in these families.

Benjamin Baldwin's father was born in Woburn, Massachusetts on Feb. 20, 1672/3. He settled in Canterbury, Connecticut about 1704 and died there on Dec. 11, 1759.

The wife of Hannah (Knowlton) Baldwin's great grandson, Hannah (Burnham) Baldwin might have made some repairs to the rug after her marriage into the Baldwin family on Sept 10, 1811. She was one of many in the family with the initials H.B. and she would have initialed her sheets both before and after her marriage with H.B. The bed rug would have seen nearly 70 years of service in the family by this time.

The Baldwin family remained in Canterbury for many generations on the land first settled by Benjamin Baldwin in 1704. A notation in family papers mentioned the purchase of the Canterbury land on Feb. 20, 1704 from Jedediah Fitch for £30 of silver. The land was two miles long and 60 rods, about 990 feet, wide bounded on the east by the Quinnebaug River, south by the Norwich line, north by land of Jedediah Fitch and west by property owned by Elisha Paine. The family papers also state that the land, as of May 30, 1892, was occupied by the sixth generation in regular descent from Benjamin, Benjamin, Timothy, David, Elijah, Elijah Jr. and Sarah. The original dwelling had been removed and newer homes built on the tract by 1892.

The colorful bed rug consists of a large round scalloped-edged multi-colored flower in the center of the bed cover. Trails of vines and smaller flowers surround the central motif that is set off in a square about the size of the top of a bed and outlined by two lines, one dark blue and one white.

The border of the rug also consists of vines holding many smaller flowers and leaves. A thin line of dark blue and white runs around the outside edge of the cover. Colors used to embroider the rug include deep orange, yellow, brown, green and natural. The background is a variety of medium blues.

The loop-pile running stitch was used to embroider the cover, and some of the pile was cut and other areas were left uncut. The background fabric is a woolen blanket of two breadths seamed vertically measuring approximately 85 inches long and 79 inches wide.

Old repairs were made with hand woven linen sheeting on the back of the rug, and newer embroidery stitches were added in several areas. One fascinating old repair was made by appliquéing two leaf-shaped pieces of nearly black wool worsted fabric over two areas in the upper third of the rug. These were quite unsightly and not in keeping with the embroidered surface of the rug. When the patches were removed and the underlying foundation fabric was exposed, stitch holes in the foundation fabric were conclusive evidence that the embroidery stitches had been removed. No other damage was found under the black patches. Each area of removed stitches was the perfect shape of an ovate leaf design. It appeared as if someone had intentionally removed the stitches from each of these leaf designs, and that someone not familiar with the bed rug making techniques might have done the appliqué repair.

Moths and other vermin had done their share of damage to the rug, and a person not aware of the value of bed rugs, did further damage by beating the bed cover with a rug beater as it hung on a clothesline. Fortunately an antiques enthusiast who knew the value of the old bed cover rescued it before it was demolished by the beating.

Repairs were made by applying sturdy antique hand woven linen sheeting to the back of damaged areas of the bed cover. All areas of the bed rug that had been damaged were carefully stitched down with cotton thread to the linen backing. Then new embroidery, using the loop-pile running stitch, in appropriately natural-dyed handspun yarn was made to those areas where the embroidery was missing.

The Lorraine Collins Rug

The bed rug made by Lorraine Collins in 1786 has an interesting pattern of flowers and many birds created with a variety of blues, yellows, greens, browns and natural colored yarns. It is one of the few known rugs made with the darning stitch. The maker wrote her full name and the date in cross-stitches at the top of the bed rug. The dark background of the rug differentiates it from those rugs made with the darning stitch by women in the Colchester, Connecticut area. Their rugs were stitched with a natural background and with only a few shades of blue and browns for the patterns. Collins' use of birds, more than 30, is another distinguishing feature not found in the Colchester rugs, and her overall design is more irregular than the Colchester area covers.

A large many-lobed flower with a contrasting set of sepals dominates the center of the Collins rug. Above this motif are two birds flanking the name of the maker and the date. The rug is asymmetrical but is tied together by a wandering vine, which emanates from a two-handled vase at the foot of the rug. Two large floral carnation-like motifs are on either side of the vase at the foot of the rug, and three large dissimilar floral patterns were stitched on each side of the rug. The rest of the open area is filled with smaller flowers, leaves and birds.

The dove-shaped birds were placed among the flowers and leaves, but as they are much smaller than the flowers they seem to hide in the foliage. The birds, which are depicted more realistically than the floral motifs, were outlined with a running stitch. The running stitch also was used to outline the wing as the birds are shown in profile, perched on vines and not in flight. The birds were filled in with various darning stitches in a variety of shades of blues and yellows. The wing is composed of one type of darning stitch completely different from the stitchery used to create the body of the bird. These two patterns most often ran in different directions. Lorraine Collins sometimes chose two different patterns in a single bird and varied these patterns with several shades of either blue or yellow, or a combination of blues and yellows. The overall effect was to create many kinds of birds when in reality the birds only vary in size, from six to nine inches in length. The only variation in the bird profile is that a few birds have their heads facing towards their tails.

All the flowers are different from one another with the exception of the two serrated-topped carnation-type flowers at the foot of the rug. The calyx or bud leaf of each flower was outlined in running stitch, as were the petals. The calyx was stitched in contrasting color from the main part of the flower. The flower colors consist of three shades of blue, three shades of yellow, yellow-orange, and tan.

One especially interesting motif looks like a cross section of an orange with bright yellow-orange stitches. Interspersed within the large flowers, smaller blooms, birds, leaves and vines, are many round, orange-colored fruits. Several motifs were stitched in bright blue accented with lighter blues, and two sets of clover-like dark blue leaves were set on either side of the vase at the foot of the rug. All the designs were emphasized by the brown background also made with the darning stitch.

31

The lower corners of the rug were cut away some time after the rug was made presumably to use the rug on a tall post bed. The top of the rug also appears to have been cut off, perhaps because of excessive wear at this edge, which would have been handled daily while making up the bed.

The rug is now 88 inches long and 92 inches wide and is constructed on a woolen blanket, made up of three sections, 36, 38 and 18 inches wide. The blanket was woven with 18 ends per inch in both the warp and the weft. The coarse but even weave helped the maker count the threads for construction of the darning stitches as she filled in the motifs.

The rug, discovered in 1982 in Vermont, and owned by the Renate Halpern Galleries of New York City, might at one time have been used as a floor rug because the pattern of wear is evident around the outside edges as if it had been set on the floor with a table in the center. Another rug found in Rhode Island had similar wear and was also thought to have been used as a floor rug once it was no longer thought suitable as a bedspread.

Many rugs suffered from misuse and neglect over the years. Some were used as horse blankets, were found discarded in barns, were subject to moth and mice damage, were cut off at the corners or along the top, and some were cut off at the sides. One was cut in half and used as an underlayment for a new floor carpet, was later found and repaired, and is now at the New York Historical Society in New York City. This rug, attributed to Sarah (Griswold) Hyde, is discussed in a later chapter.

Some repairs to rugs have been poorly executed by not following the original needle techniques. Some were repaired using the hooking technique rather than embroidery, as the repairer thought the rug had been hooked. One rug has had a new upper edge replaced by using a linen background unlike the wool background of the original rug. The embroidery in this repair is not as well executed as the original; the woolen yarns and the patterns used do not match the original rug.

Molly Lothrop's Bed Rug

The original owner of this rug, Molly Stark Lothrop, born in 1752, was a daughter of General John Stark's brother. She married James Lothrop in 1773 at age 21 and went to live with him in Bennington, Vermont.

Her aunt, Molly Stark, wife of General Stark, famous military officer in the French and Indian War as well as the American Revolution, made the rug for her niece and namesake. Although she really was her niece, Molly Stark was really not her name. According to family records, Mrs. Stark's maiden name was Elizabeth Page, and her husband, the general, who had a liking for nicknames, affixed his wife with the nickname of Molly. All of his eleven children also were called by nicknames. In addition, General Stark renamed Molly Stark, his niece, to Polly Stark.

General and Molly Stark lived in Derryfield, New Hampshire, now known as Manchester. Their farm, which also contained a mill, was left to Molly to run during the General's absence throughout the Revolutionary War. The general distinguished himself at the battle of Bunker Hill as he had done in the French and Indian War 25 years earlier.

At the time of Molly Stark Lothrop's wedding to James Lothrop, family tradition said that the aunt, Molly, made the bed rug. The pattern Molly Stark used is typical of the third quarter 18th century rugs with a large floral bouquet rising out of a group of leaves at the base of the rug, complemented by a vine containing large flowers, that ran around the outer edges of the cover.

The rug measures 73 inches in length by 83 ½ inches in width. It is constructed on a tabby weave, natural color wool foundation, which contained two sections seamed vertically. The embroidery is fashioned with the running stitch with an uncut pile and depicts a trailing leaf design, carnations, small flowers and berries. The central motif is a large carnation. The colors of the rug run from light beige to chocolate brown. A part of the right edge and a portion of the foot of the rug have been cut away. The rug has been backed.

The family preserved the rug for many generations. Mrs. Belle Case, a great-granddaughter of the original owner gave the bed cover to the Society of the Daughters of the American Revolution Museum, Washington, D.C. in 1922. Mrs. Case was a member of the Louis Joliet Chapter of the DAR in Joliet, Illinois.

The Esther Lyman Rug

The 1771 bed rug made by Esther Lyman (1750-1828) of Coventry, Connecticut was stitched when the maker was 21 years old. She was married to Stephen Howard of Tolland, Connecticut in 1782, when she was 32 years old. The rug descended through the family, and was donated to the Connecticut Historical Society in Hartford in 1963 by a descendant.

The rug is constructed on a wool background of natural color with brown stripes. Esther Lyman did not use the pattern of the background material as an aid to her pattern embroidery as several other rug makers had. The background blanket consists of three widths of fabric, a 16-inch section and two 33-inch sections, seamed vertically.

The rug is embroidered with the running stitch, which was then cut to make a pile effect, a practice used by other bed rug makers. The colors consist of browns, gold, natural color and several shades of blue upon a background of green embroidery. The rug is 86 inches in length and 80 inches wide.

The pattern consists of three very large flowers. All the vines and flowers emanate from one of these large flowers at the bottom center of the rug. Above this central flower is a smaller floral motif unattached to the vines. At the head of the rug is the date, 1771 under the initials E L. The yarns used to embroider the rug varied in thickness. She used more strands of thinner, colored yarns, and fewer strands of the thicker, natural color yarn when constructing the bed cover.

Esther Lyman was the daughter of Dr. Elijah Lyman, who was tenth child of Jonathan and Lydia (Loomis) Lyman of Lebanon, Connecticut. A physician, Dr. Lyman married Esther Clark (1730-1818), daughter of Gershom and Esther (Strong) Clark also of Lebanon. Dr. and Mrs. Lyman resided in Coventry on a road now known as Bread and Milk Street. They had three children, Esther, born July 4, 1750; Gershom, born in 1752; and Lucy, who was born July 16, 1756, married Dr. John Waldo.

Stephen Howard, husband of Esther Lyman was born in 1747. According to family papers, he is the son of Nathaniel Howard, born in 1718 in Steventown, New York. Nathaniel fought in the battle of Saratoga, New York, in 1771 died Oct. 20, 1777, age 59, in Steventown. Stephen Howard was listed in *Men of the Revolution* (Connecticut) as serving eight days in answer to the Lexington Alarm.

Stephen and Esther (Lyman) Howard had two children, Elizabeth Howard (1790-1888) and Esther Howard. Esther Howard married Deacon Selah Loomis of Coventry.

Stephen Howard disappeared from his home in 1796. At this time, Esther then 46 years old, went to her parent's home to reside with her widowed mother. Eleven years later on May 4, 1807 Mrs. Lyman sold the family farm in Coventry, and the two women moved to Vermont to live with their son and brother, the Rev. Gershom Lyman. The Rev. Lyman died April 13, 1813 in Marlborough, Vermont at age 61. He had been minister for 35 years of the Marlborough Congregational Church, the church's first pastor. Upon his death, the two women moved back to Coventry, where they lived with the bed rug maker's daughter, Esther (Howard) Loomis, and her husband, Deacon Selah Loomis, on a road now known as Love Lane. Esther (Lyman) Howard died in 1828. Her mother had died in 1818.

Sarah Woodward Waterman Rug

Sarah Woodward, maker of a colorful bed rug in 1794, was born on May 31, 1747 in Mansfield, Connecticut and died at Norwich, Vermont. Oct. 31, 1827 at the age of 80. She was the daughter of Deliverance and Abigail (Jewell) Woodward. She married Lt. Samuel Waterman on February 25, 1771. Waterman was born on Feb. 15, 1746 in Bozrah, Connecticut and died on August 29, 1809 in Norwich, Vermont according to his gravestone.

At one time it was thought that Sarah and Samuel's daughter, Sabre made the bed rug but she would have been only six years old when the rug was made. Sabre was born in 1788 in Norwich, Connecticut. She was the seventh child of this couple.

The rug made by Sarah is stitched on a dark woolen, plain weave foundation and is 89 by 97 inches. The rounded corners at the foot of the rug were fashioned in this shape when the rug was made. Later owners of some rugs cut the lower corners to fit high post beds, and this is obvious by observing the missing pattern elements on these rugs. The Waterman rug has a scalloped design running around the two sides and the foot of the cover. A large central motif with a leafy-vase is located at the base of the cover from which large vines encircle the rug and hold many flowers and leaves. The initials and date are at the top of the rug. The rug is made of blue, tan and yellow on a sepia background. It was sewn with the running stitch with both cut and uncut pile and is now at the Smithsonian Institution, The National Museum of History and Technology.

1. The Mary Avery 1722 bed rug *(above)*. See page 37. Courtesy Peabody Essex Museum, Salem, Mass.
2. A Welsh, single-color bed rug *(below)*. See page 52. Courtesy National Museum of Wales.

3. The Bowne bed rug (*above*). See page 39. Courtesy of Colonial Williamsburg Foundation.
4. The Esther Lyman bed rug (*below*). See page 34. Courtesy of Connecticut Historical Society, Hartford, CT.

5. A Connecticut River Valley bed rug, F-416 (*above*). See page 27. Collection of Historic Deerfield Inc.
6. Hannah Pearl bed rug (*below*). See page 39. Courtesy Wadsworth Atheneum, Hartford, lent by Miss Isabel Rogers.

7. Mary Comstock bed rug (*above*). See page 42. © Courtesy Shelburne Museum, Shelburne, Vermont
8. Patience (Foote) Brainerd, (*below*) maker of the bed rug shown in Plate 9. See page 28.

PATIENCE (FOOTE) BRAINERD.

9. Patience (Foote) Brainerd made this bed rug (*above*) before her marriage. See page 28.
10. Rebekah Hale rug (*below*). See page 24. Courtesy of National Museum of American History Smithsonian Institution.

11. The Elizabeth Foote bed rug (*above*). See page 26. Courtesy Connecticut Historical Society, Hartford, Ct.
12. Detail of the Elizabeth Foote bed rug (*below*). Courtesy Connecticut Historical Society, Hartford, Ct.

13. The Lorraine Collins bed rug (*above*). See page 31. Courtesy Renate Halpern Galleries Inc., New York, NY.
14. New England bed rug (*below*). See page 43. Courtesy Antiquarian & Landmark Society Inc. of Connecticut.

15. Sarah Waterman rug (*above*). See page 36. Courtesy National Museum of American History Smithsonian Institution.
16. A Southern bed rug (*below*). See page 44. Collection of the Museum of Early Southern Decorative Arts.

More Bed Rugs

While the list of bed rug makers can never be complete, the women who made the covers would be pleased to know that at least some of their efforts at creating an imaginative and useful decoration for their home have survived, and more important, that they are regarded today as works of art.

Among the rug makers now known is **Mary Avery** of North Andover, Massachusetts, who initialed her rug M A, and dated it 1722. This rug is the earliest known dated rug, and is located at Peabody Essex Museum, Salem, Massachusetts. It was made on a natural wool foundation two breadths wide, and executed with the running stitch with cut pile in dark brown, dark blue, gold and natural. Repairs to the rug have added light brown, red and green. It appears that the lower corners have been cut away, so that it would fit more easily around bedposts.

Sources believe that **Catherine Thorn** made the bed rug that is dated 1724 and initialed it C T. Catherine probably made it for her sister, Mary Thorn, as a wedding gift. They were daughters of Deacon Thorn of Ipswich, Massachusetts. Mary was married to Richard Dodge, son of William Dodge of Wenham, Massachusetts on Nov. 16, 1724 and died in 1730. Catherine Thorn married Francis King in 1728. It is also possible that Deacon Thorn's wife, whose name might have been Catherine, made the cover for her daughter, Mary. This rug is located at Wenham Historical Association & Museum, Wenham, Massachusetts.

A bed rug dated 1741 and inscribed with the initials B over E P was probably made by **Phoebe (Denison) Billings** (1690-1775), daughter of John Borodell Denison and Phebe (Lay) Denison. John Borodell Denison was born on June 14, 1646 in Roxbury, Massachusetts and died in 1697 in Stonington, Connecticut. Her mother was born Jan. 5, 1651 in Saybrook and died in 1699 in Stonington. They were married Nov. 26, 1667.

John Borodell Denison was the son of Capt. George Denison, who was born Dec. 6, 1620 in Bishop's Stortford, Hertfordshire, England and died Oct. 23 1694 in Hartford, Connecticut. He is buried in the Old Center Church burial ground in Hartford. Capt. Denison married Ann Borodell who was born May 17, 1615 in Cork, Ireland and died Sept. 26, 1712 in Stonington. She is buried in Elm Grove Cemetery, Mystic, Connecticut. Phebe Lay was the daughter of Robert Lay, born in 1617 in England and died July 9, 1689 in Saybrook, and Sarah (Fenner) Lay, born in 1616 in England and died May 25, 1676 in Saybrook. Sarah (Fenner) Lay was the daughter of Arthur Fenner, born in Horley, Sussex, England, who died in 1647 in Branford, Massachusetts, and Sarah (Browne) Fenner.

Phoebe Denison married Ebenezer Billings Jr. on April 2, 1706. He was born Jan. 1, 1684 in Stonington, baptized May 11, 1690 in Stonington and died in Stonington July 20, 1760. Ebenezer Billings Jr. was the son of Ebenezer Billings, born in 1661, died Sept. 16, 1727 in Stonington and is buried in North Stonington, and Anna (Comstock) Billings, who was born in 1661 in Norwich, Connecticut and died Oct. 5, 1727 in Stonington. The couple was married March 1, 1680/81 in Stonington.

Ebenezer Billings (Sr.) was the son of William Billings and Mary (Atherton) Billings. He was born 1629 in Taunton, Somersetshire, England and died March 16, 1713 in Stonington. They were married May 12, 1657 in Dorchester, Massachusetts. Mary died on Block Island, Rhode Island. in 1718. William Billings' father, William Billings was born in 1601 in Taunton, England. His parents were Richard and Elizabeth (Strong) Billings both of England.

Anna (Comstock) Billings, daughter of Daniel Comstock and Paltiah (Elderkin) Comstock, was baptized in Norwich on April 9, 1671 and died Oct. 5, 1727 in Stonington. Anna Comstock's father was born July 21, 1630 in Culmstock, Devonshire, England and died in 1683 in New London, Connecticut. Her mother, Paltiah (Elderkin) Comstock was born in 1632 in Norwich and died after Feb. 21 in 1713 in Connecticut. Daniel Comstock was the son of William Comstock and Elizabeth (Daniel) Comstock. He was born in 1595 in St. Martin's in Fields, London and died in 1683 in New London. Elizabeth was born in 1625 in England and died about 1663 in New London. Paltiah Elderkin was the daughter of John Elderkin, born in 1612 and died June 13, 1687, and Abigail (Kingsland) Elderkin who died before 1660.

It is interesting to note that Anna Comstock's father, Daniel Comstock, and the husband of bed rug maker, Mary Comstock, who was also named Daniel Comstock, both came from New London. These men lived in different centuries, but the families were undoubtedly related.

The Phoebe (Denison) Billings bed rug was stitched with a running stitch with uncut pile in cream, tan, and gold. The center background was black, and the border background was dark blue. The rug is 96 inches square and is artistically designed with a meandering floral vine placed around the outside border, and several large flowers are placed in the center on either side of the date and initials. A serpentine multi-colored band quite different from any other bed rug separates the two sections. This design is similar to the M and W design featured in the Elizabeth Townshend 1815 manuscript of embroidery designs. The rug is owned by Addison Gallery of American Art, Phillips Academy, Andover, Massachusetts.

A colorful bed rug, whose maker is unknown, was probably stitched in the mid 18th century in the southern Maine. It is owned by the Old York Historical Society, York, Maine, and is pictured on the cover of this book. The rug is constructed on a natural wool foundation of tabby weave and created with a running stitch with cut and uncut pile. The colors are gold, brown, cream and tan on a light blue background. The rug is 72 inches long and 85 ½ inches wide and the foot of the rug may have been cut off at one time.

Mary (Hinkley) West (1715-1794) probably made the bed rug that was initialed W over N M and dated 1763. She married Nathan West (1712-1801) in 1738. The bed rug, made 25 years after her marriage, was embroidered using the tree of life design with the running stitch with uncut pile with yarns in green, brown and gold on a blue background. It is stitched on a natural wool foundation and is 95 inches long and 87 ½ inches wide with rounded corners at the foot of the spread. Captain Elias West, son of Nathan and Mary (Hinkley) West was born July 5, 1744 and served in the Revolutionary

War. He married Mary Luthrop of Norwich and their daughter, Zerviah West, born Nov. 10, 1773 married Gurdon Gifford who was born July 3, 1768 and died Nov. 11, 1850. Zerviah died Dec. 3, 1795. The rug descended in the family to Frederick William Weir (1860-1929) through his mother Eliza Gifford who was married to the Rev. John Weir, and thence to his cousins in the Thayer/Taintor family. It is located at the Addison Gallery of American Art.

With a Long Island, New York provenance, a rug now owned by Colonial Williamsburg Foundation was probably made in the third quarter of the 18th century. It belonged to the F.S. Bowne family of Flushing, New York and descended through the Draper family. The tree of life design was executed with darning, long and short and outline stitches in four shades of blue, three shades of gold, amber and blue-green on natural background. The piece is finished with a natural colored fringe. A seven-inch strip of linen was added across the top of the rug some time after the bed cover was made. The embroidery and colors on this strip do not match the original bed cover. The size of the rug is 79 inches long and 97 inches wide.

Deborah (Loomis) Brace (1752-1839) was married to Ariel Brace of Torrington, Connecticut in 1771 or 1772. She stitched a very colorful bed rug and initialed it DB with two Xs standing for her age of 20. She also dated the rug 1772. The rug, stitched on a natural wool foundation, is 87 inches long and 86 inches wide, and embroidered with the running stitch with cut pile in tan, cream, olive green, dark blue, red and white on a medium blue background. It has olive green fringe. It is designed with a central square in which a shell-like vase holds vines full of flowers. A floral vine winds around the entire border from the foot to the head of the spread. A scalloped border runs along the outer edge. This rug is located at Yale University Art Gallery.

A rug at the Governor Jonathan Trumbull House in Lebanon, Connecticut owned by the Connecticut Daughters of the American Revolution is dated 1764 and might have been made by a member of the Geer family. It is initialed MG at the head of the cover near the date. The cover, 86 inches square, features the tree of life design stitched with the running stitch with uncut pile in shades of dark olive green, saffron, three shades of blue and one of yellow on a cream background. The foundation consists of natural wool made of two and one half breadths seamed vertically. An undulating scalloped border surrounds the two sides and the foot of the cover. The lower corners were rounded at the time the rug was made

A rug made in the last quarter of the 18th century was signed with the maker's full name, **Hannah Pearl**. It is thought to have come from the Pomfret-Hampton, Connecticut area, but it has been impossible to discover which Hannah made the rug as several by that name were living in that area during that period of time. The 82-inch long by 90-inch wide rug is made entirely with the stem stitch in three shades of blue on a cream background. The embroidery was worked on a natural wool foundation. Wadsworth Atheneum owns the rug.

Dated 1779, a rug initialed E H was probably made by **Sarah (Griswold) Hyde**. Family tradition said it was made for Elihu Hyde of Chelsea, Vermont, son of the maker but it more likely was made for her husband, Elihu. The couple was married March 2,

1766 in Norwich, Connecticut according to Norwich Vital Records. They had three sons, Elihu, born June 2, 1767, Asaph, born March 1769 and Richard, born June 4, 1772. Sarah (Griswold) Hyde was the daughter of Joseph Griswold and Sarah (Durkee) Hyde. Elihu Hyde (Sr.) was born March 3, 1734 and died Oct. 9, 1815 in New Hampshire according to the DAR Index of Patriotic Service.

The rug was at one time cut in half and placed under a carpet as padding. It was found in the late 1920s and restored. An article in the magazine *Antiques* in November 1927 tells of its rescue, and also erroneously described the rug as hooked. An illustration in that issue before the rug's restoration showed the uneven horizontal cut. The rug was constructed on a natural wool foundation 95 inches long by 89 inches wide using running stitches with both cut and uncut pile. The blue, green and tan designs were placed on an undyed background. The pattern of the rug was the popular branching floral bush surrounded by a serpentine vine holding floral motifs. The initials and date are in the center at the head of the cover. This rug is at the New York Historical Society, New York City.

Bed rug maker **Eunice (Williams) Metcalf** of Lebanon, who was born in 1775, was probably related to, and knew bed rug maker, Philena McCall of Lebanon. Eunice Metcalf's rug dates from 1790-1800. Family tradition called the rug "grandpa's old rug". Stitched on a natural wool foundation with the popular running stitch with cut pile, the maker used shades of rust red, gray and olive green on a yellow-beige background. The rug, 94 ½ inches long and 80 ½ inches wide, featured rounded corners at the foot of the spread that were done at the time of construction. An olive green fringe surrounds the sides and lower edge. A discussion of the McCall bed rug, owned by Wadsworth Atheneum, is found in the Hale Family Bed Rugs chapter.

Two very similar rugs, probably from the Norwich/New London area, with bold geometrical designs stand out from all the other bed covers because of their deep colors and their intricate design. At the head of the covers are cartouches with initials and dates. The earlier rug is designed with a shell pattern in the center of the rug with a cartouche at the center top flanked by bold star-like designs. The border consists of wavy jagged lines running around the sides and foot of the rug. The colors are shades of blue with white and dark brown. The initials are W over R B and the date is 1783. The later rug dated 1790 has a similar border but the shell center is outlined with a bold scallop design. The cartouche at the head of the bed is placed on top of a branching leafy motif. The initials E over R G and the date are placed in the cartouche. The colors are three shades of blue and white. Both covers, stitched with the running stitch with uncut pile, have rounded ends at the foot of the bed rug made during construction. They are both made on natural wool foundations and of similar size. The 1783 rug is 90 inches long and 87 inches wide, and the 1790 rug is 87 inches long and 88 ½ inches wide. The 1783 rug is now at the Henry Francis du Pont Winterthur Museum, and the 1790 rug is at The Brooklyn Museum.

Another very different bed rug is located in New Brunswick, Canada. It was probably made between 1790 and 1810 and constructed on a natural wool foundation with a technique referred to as double stitched pile. This is made by working the double stitch across the foundation fabric changing colors to accommodate the pattern. The stitching is different from any of the other bed rugs known at this time. Colors used by the unknown maker were light and dark blue, dark blue-green, golden yellows, light brown and terra cotta on an undyed background. The size is 87 inches long and 62 inches wide. The rug is at The New Brunswick Museum in St. John.

Two rugs with Colchester histories were each dated 1796 in the embroidery. The first is initialed N L and was acquired from the Jonathan Deming House in Colchester. It is now owned by the Metropolitan Museum of Art. This rug is stitched in the running stitch with both cut and uncut pile in brown, tan, green and gold on an undyed, natural background. It is 94 inches long and 90 inches wide. The second 1796 rug is initialed H J and is believed to have been made by **Hannah Johnson** (1770-1818), daughter of Ebenezer and Anna Johnson of Bozrah, Connecticut, a town on the eastern border of Colchester. The number 26, also embroidered on the rug would indicate her age at the time the rug was made. Hannah was never married. The rug is made on a natural wool foundation with the running stitch with uncut pile in shades of golden yellow, brown, green, blue and rose on an undyed background. The size is 98 inches long and 94 inches wide. According to family tradition, a niece of Hannah Johnson, also named Hannah, who died in 1850, inherited the rug, and she passed it on to her daughter, Mrs. W. H. Sterling. The family moved to New York State from Connecticut at some time in the 19th century. The rug is located at the Art Institute of Chicago.

The pattern of both rugs is the popular winding floral vine emerging from a double-handled vase surrounding the center that features a bouquet rising out of a second double-handled vase. Many carnation-like flowers are used in both rugs along with flowers with ovate looped petals. Interspersed throughout the rugs are smaller flowers and some of the vines are feathered at the foot of the rugs. Although each rug is different, at first glance they seem the same. Though the designs are similar to the Foote family rugs, also made in the Colchester area, they appear dissimilar due to the different embroidery stitches and choice of yarn colors.

A lively rug with giant flowers in each corner and three more across the center was stitched with the running stitch with both cut and uncut pile. The rug is attributed to a maker with the initials E S. Those initials are stitched in the upper right portion of the rug. To the left is the name **Sara Denny** presumably for whom the rug was made between 1800 and 1825. The embroidery was made in shades of green, blue, yellow, tan, light brown and rose on an undyed background. A scalloped border surrounds the entire rug, which is located at Shelburne Museum, Shelburne, Vermont.

Research into genealogical documents has uncovered an Elizabeth Spooner who married David Denny in 1790. They resided in Northfield, Vermont. One of their nine children was Sarah Denny born Nov. 6, 1800. The bed rug could have been made by or for Sarah. It also could have been started by Elizabeth Spooner and finished by Sarah or possibly someone else. The name Sarah is stitched on the rug as Sara, but there is a space where the missing H could have been inscribed at one time. Since the rug has had much reworking both the name and the initials could have been added or changed while that repairing was done.

David Denny originally came from Leicester, Massachusetts, and his father, Samuel, had served as an officer in the Revolutionary War. Elizabeth Spooner was the oldest child of Paul and Aseneth (Wright) Spooner, who were married in 1769. Aseneth (Wright) Spooner was the daughter of Amasa Wright.

Mary (Bishop) Comstock stitched a remarkable rug and dated it January 30, 1810. Born in Norwich, Connecticut in 1744, she made the bed cover when she was 66 years old. Mary and her husband, Daniel (1742-1816) moved from Connecticut to Vermont in 1770, first to Sunderland and then about 1784 to Shelburne (Comstock Point). She died May 7, 1828 at age 84. Daniel was the son of Peter Comstock and Martha (Avery) Comstock. The rug was made with the running stitch on a plaid woolen foundation fabric. Blue, tan and brown stitches are set off by a dark brown and black stitched background. The cover features a single, very large motif consisting of a vase at the base of the rug from which several flowers and vines arise. A scalloped border runs around the sides and curved foot of the rug. Mary's name and the date are stitched in large letters across the entire top of the rug. The rug is at Shelburne Museum.

Another group of rugs remain unidentified but some contain initials that someday may lead to the maker's names. The earliest in this group is the knotted pile rug, made while the rug was in the loom and dated 1741 or 1743, and initialed I A S. The rug is geometric in pattern with a wide herringbone border, and a smaller herringbone border outlines the center of the rug that contains a large diamond. Each motif is made with several shades of green, yellow and cream on a dark blue background. The size is 76 inches by 73 inches and the knots are worked on a natural wool foundation. Cross-stitched into the foundation with red wool is the almost indiscernible date. This rug is located at the Faith Trumbull Chapter, Daughters of the American Revolution Museum and Chapter House in Norwich, Connecticut.

A rug stitched with three shades of beige on a blue and green background in the running stitch is dated 1748 and initialed either E B or F B. It might have been made in Massachusetts. A rug initialed L P or L T made about 1790-1800 was constructed in two shades of blue on a cream ground by using the running stitch with uncut pile on the wool foundation. It is at New York State Historical Association, Cooperstown, New York.

Another rug with a provenance of the Connecticut River Valley has no identifying marks. It is constructed with the darning stitch, with curved stitches for creating the motifs and straight stitches for the dark brown background. The designs are worked in shades of yellow, orange and light blue. Brown and blue fringe surround the sides and foot of the cover. Among the many flowers and vines that spring from a leafy base are numerous birds. A large carnation like flower dominates the center of the rug. This rug is at Historic Deerfield Inc., Massachusetts.

An unidentified rug but with a Connecticut River Valley provenance has the initials E B and was most likely made between 1790 and 1800. It is constructed with the running stitch with cut pile and features the popular double-handled vase holding a bouquet of large flowers surrounded by wandering vines and flowers stemming from a branching leafy base. A part of the left side and lower edge have been cut away. This rug is also at Historic Deerfield Inc.

A wonderful and uniquely designed bed rug with three large flowerpots across the lower center of the rug has retained much color. The center pot contains a gigantic, many lobed, circular, multi-hued flower, and the outer pots hold trailing vines and flowers. The border features alternating leaves and cabbage rose motifs. This rug, 90 inches long and 83 inches wide is made with the running stitch with cut pile in shades of tan, rose, yellow, violet and dark green on an undyed background. Although unidentified, the bed cover has been given a northern New England provenance and an early 19th century construction date. The rug is owned by the Antiquarian and Landmark Society of Connecticut and is on display at the Joshua Hempsted House in New London, Connecticut.

Two rugs of similar design, featuring the popular two-handled vase holding a bouquet at the center of the rug surrounded by a feathered vine and large floral carnation like motifs, remain unidentified. The earlier rug is initialed E L and dated 1807. The other is dated 1809 and is initialed M B. They were probably made in the Connecticut River Valley. Both are embroidered with the running stitch with cut pile and both have dark backgrounds and polychrome motifs. The 1807 rug measures 100 inches long by 94 inches wide and is at the Shelburne Museum. The 1809 rug is 102 ½ inches long and 97 inches wide and is at the Metropolitan Museum of Art. Later bed rugs were generally larger than earlier rugs.

Two rugs were made with more realistic looking flowers and fruit than many of the earlier rugs. The first is dated 1819 and initialed illegibly, but possibly with the letters N C. The running stitch with uncut pile with shades of blue, brown and beige on an undyed background delineate many well-executed motifs including grapes, pineapples, cherries, raspberries and a wide variety of flowers. The central bouquet rises out of a leafy base, as does the floral vine that winds around the border. The lower corners appear to have been rounded some time after the bed rug was completed. The provenance is unknown. This rug is at Henry Francis duPont Winterthur Museum.

A bed rug dated 1821 and initialed L M is also made with realistic motifs, including strawberries, grapes and cherries and a variety of life-like flowers. The design also features the central bouquet rising from a leafy base and a border of floral vines emanating from a larger leafy base. A well designed and intricate, triple-shaded, scalloped pattern was stitched between the border and the dark fringe. The colors in the rug are yellow, buff and three shades of green on a brown and black background. The rug measures 108 inches long and 102 inches wide. The rug was found in southern New Hampshire and was owned for many years by Bertram K. and Nina Fletcher Little. It is now part of the collection of the Society for the Preservation of New England Antiquities.

A bed rug, in two fragments, with the date 1833 and initialed H M has the distinction of being the latest known bed rug. Nothing more is known about this bed cover. The rug was constructed on a natural wool foundation with the running stitch in polychrome yarns on a brown background. These fragments are located at the American Museum in Britain, Claverton Manor, Bath, England.

Bed Rugs of Southern
And Other Atlantic Coastal Areas

Bed rugs were found in inventories in the southern states and in the middle states as well. They were often listed with other bedding and were spelled both rug and rugg. The covers were rarely called bed rugs, but were sometimes referred to as rug coverlets, shag rugs or Irish rugs. Some inventories made note of the color of the rugs including green, red, blue and gray. They appear in inventories from the 1600 through 1800 and after that fewer and fewer mention of rugs is made. Other types of bedding in these inventories were coverlets, quilts, counterpanes, and blankets. It is difficult to tell from the insufficient information given in wills and inventories to ascertain if the bed rugs were imported or American made. What is important is that rugs, whether made here or abroad, were an important enough item to be mentioned in a will, as well as part of an estate's inventory throughout this area of the country, as well as in New England.

The inventory of the estate of Mrs. Eve Smith, taken Dec. 5, 1705 at the home of Abraham Goad, included three featherbeds, curtains, valences and all furniture, one featherbed and bolster, two pillows, one flock bed, a rug, bolster, blanket, and three pair of sheets. This was recorded in Richmond County, Virginia. When the word rug is found among other bedding it can be assumed that the inventory maker was referring to a type of bed furnishing. A flock bed was a mattress made with scraps of wool fleece, which were portions of the fleece too damaged or too short to be spun into yarn.

A bed rug, now at the Museum of Early Southern Decorative Arts in Winston Salem, North Carolina, is probably American made and has a Wytheville, Virginia provenance. It was fashioned on a twill weave wool and linen foundation, made of two breadths and is 89 ¾ inches long and 73 ¾ inches wide. The rug is initialed E G in one corner and 825 in another corner. As the rug appears to have been cut off at this point, it is safe to assume the 1 from the date 1825 is missing.

The rug was produced with turkey work knots in a geometric pattern. The knots were probably worked while the fabric was on the loom, as the two sections do not match where they meet at the center seam. The center section of the rug is a series of diamonds within octagons and the colors in this area include dark blue, light blue and brown. The border is a zigzag or flame stitch pattern similar to the 1722 Mary Avery rug at Peabody Essex Museum, Salem, Massachusetts and the 1741/43 bed rug located at Faith Trumbull Museum in Norwich, Connecticut. The border pattern of the Virginia rug is worked with olive green, light blue and brown yarns.

The pile of the rug, made by the knots has almost completely worn away but sources believe the pile originally was nearly 1½-inches long. The knots were made with three 2-ply yarns. Most northern bed rugs used several strands of single ply yarn for both embroidered and knotted rugs. The knots in the southern rug were made around every 11th and 12th warp end across one row followed by six rows of brown wool weft. This pattern of knots and plain weave was used throughout the rug.

In Hyde County, North Carolina, a seacoast area, Sarah White, widow, left a 'great' rug in her will dated January 26, 1726. Henry Eborn in a document dated Oct. 20, 1732 willed his daughter Rhoda Layson, a bed, two sheets, two blankets, a rug and bolster. Her sisters, Mary Eborn and Elizabeth Eborn were each left beds and a rug among other bed furnishings. In a will dated November 11, 1751, Simon Foscue, planter, also from Hyde County left his eldest son, Richard, a feather bed and bolster, sheet, blanket and rug. His second son, Simon, was willed a homespun jacket and breeches, one feather bed, bolster, sheet and blanket. However his daughter Sarah Sanderson and his son, Bell each received feather beds, bedding and rugs.

Sabastian Silverthorn, whose will was dated December 22, 1751 in Hyde County, North Carolina, left rugs among other bedding to his son John and to his daughter, Lydia. He also referred to a daughter called Mary but christened Lydia and to a daughter, Agness. He left some bedding but no rugs to a daughter Sary and also to an unborn child. Silverthorn left to John Change "one bed tick when he gets feathers to fill it and if he Stays with my wife and burns the Lightwood that I heapt up, I give him a Coat and Briches of Duroys and a jacket of Good homespunn, one blanket, one Rugg, one sheet...." It appears that John Change was a family servant, who was being paid in advance through this will, to continue to work for the family.

Three rugs were mentioned in the will left by Morris Jones of Hyde County that was dated September 1756. Bolsters were often mentioned in Hyde county wills along with blankets, sheets and quilts. Also in Hyde County, James Arthur left his daughter, Mary Arthur, "her chaus (choice) of two rugs" in his December 1773 will, and William Barrow left his son, Fredrick a feather bed, one rug and blanket, "a bolster pillo and a pare of sheets" in his April 1746 will. For the most part, wills did not contain itemized bedding but only mentioned the bed and furniture. Furniture was the word used by 18th century inventory takers and lawyers for bed clothing. Sometimes legatees were left a feather bed and furniture or bedstead and furniture. Feather beds must have been valuable and they were frequently a part of the dower of the daughters in a family. Many times the sons in a family were also left bedding in a will.

In Bath County, North Carolina, (a county started in 1696 and discontinued in 1739) George Hill left his wife Mary, "the feather bed and bolster that was hirs, also one red rug which was mine and other furniture there to belonging..." To his daughter Rachel he gave a feather bed, bolster, rug, sheets and pillow. The inventory of the "goods and chattels" of Berthese Boyd made on November 12, 1810 included two rugs among blankets, sheets and pillows.

In three inventories in the first decade of the 19th century rose blankets were mentioned. A chapter is devoted to this type of decorated blanket later in the book In a will dated 1814 in the Bath county Mary Smaw left her daughter a counterpane along with other bedding, and in 1823 an inventory of the property of Jasper Robason mentioned two quilts. No bed rugs were mentioned in the above wills and inventories.

Out of 27 different wills recorded in Craven County, North Carolina in the 18th century only one mentioned a rug, and that was in the will of Francis Stringer. He left his wife Mary Stringer, among other items, one of the best featherbeds, one good rug and one good pair of blankets (see Appendix).

Peter Guerant of Cumberland County, Virginia, who was born in 1697 in France, died in 1750 in Virginia. In his detailed and lengthy will he gave great amounts of acreage to his children including his daughters. One daughter, Esther Guerant received 200 acres of land and "the other new bed with what furniture there is to it, and a rug, and two cows and calves for her and her heirs forever, and two pounds of current money, and the two cows and calves to be delivered when she shall attain the age of twenty-one years or married" (see Appendix).

The Lunenburg County, Virginia Will Book No. 1 for 1746 to1763 includes 119 accounts and inventories and 91 wills. Some of the accounts and inventories are related to wills of that period, while others are separate entries. The most frequently mentioned items are feather beds and furniture, followed by items of clothing. No coverlets were mentioned and quilts were seldom listed.

In the will of Elizabeth Stokes of Brunswick, Virginia, probated in Lunenburg County on Oct. 1, 1751, she bequeathed her son, Richard Stokes one rug valued at 20 shillings and one sheet. The rest of her estate was given to her son, David Stokes. The will is located on page 42 of the will book. In the inventory of the estate of Daniel Firth, on Page 121 of the will book, among the items mentioned are one bed and furniture, one feather bed with bolster, two pillows, a rug, a blanket and two sheets. The entire inventory is in the Appendix. Also in the Appendix is the will of Joseph Holmes signed December 17, 1761 in which he gives a rug among other items to his nephew.

John Tennison's will dated 1682 in St. Mary's County, Maryland mentioned that his serving maid, Gressell Dongin was to receive "for her faithfulness & care in ye time of her Service and Sence bee allowed & delivered her one Cow & Calfe and 2000 lbs. of tob. (tobacco) 1 feather bed bolst'r worsted Rugg pillow & a p'r of blanketts, 1 large pewter dish & 2 larg pewter basons, 2 pewter plates, 2 pewter poring'es & 10 y'rd of hair Camelett which I have now in ye house as soone as convenient after my decease or if not ye particular things aformencenced then in lew of them to have tenn thousand pounds of tob. more that what Tob. is already menconed."

Gabriel Cooper left his son Thomas Cooper, one feather bed, bolster, one rug and a pair of blankets in his will dated February 2, 1736 in Somerset County, Maryland. Mary Marshall left "one good Rugg" a bed and other bedding to Aquila Hall, son of Aquila Hall who was a brother of her son-in-law, John Hall of Baltimore County, Maryland. John Hall was named executor of the estate. The will was dated December 23, 1745. Also in Baltimore County the will of Margaret Harvey made on January 27, 1786 among other items bequeathed to (daughter?) Abarilla Harvey a "feather Bed one pair of Sheets one Blanket one rug two pillows and Cases." To her daughter Rachel Harvey she left a feather bed, a rug, one pair of sheets, two pillows and cases.

Bed rugs were also mentioned in wills and inventories in Pennsylvania. In 1734 in the Will Book A, Volume One in Lancaster County, John Barnet stated in his will that "to my Daughter Jean one Red Coulerd (colored) and white faced Heffer Coming two year old and one rugo Or bed quilt..." (see Appendix). In the inventory of the goods and effects of James Barber made November 25, 1768 in Bristol Township, Bucks County, the following items are among many others listed. "Rugg and Blankett......00-15-00" and "a feather Bed Bedding and Bedstead......06-00-00." The rug and blanket were valued at 15 shillings and the bed and bedding at £6. These were the only bedding items mentioned. Aside from the man's wearing apparel that was valued with a horse bridle and saddle at £14, nothing else in the estate was more valuable than the bed and bedding.

While undertaking research for the restoration of the interior of the Old Barracks Museum in Trenton, New Jersey, it was found that British officers were issued bed rugs among other bedding in preparation to being sent to America in the 18th Century. This information was found in the Pennsylvania Historical Society archives. The museum has had bed rugs reproduced along with other furnishings to show how the building would have looked in the 18th century. The bed rugs, blue with red spots, were made with the knotted pile technique. The Barracks were first built in 1758 as winter quarters for British officers serving in America during the French and Indian War. British officers were quartered there for the winter when General Washington made his attack on Trenton December 26, 1776. A few years later the barracks were used as a military hospital. Similar barracks were also built in New York, Pennsylvania and South Carolina, but only the New Jersey barracks have survived.

According to the Philadelphia City Archives the inventory of Joseph Huddle of Moyamensing, Pennsylvania, taken Sept. 15, 1758, included two green rugs among other bedding.

In 136 will abstracts of residents and land owners in Long Island, New York, between 1665 and 1776 no mention of bed rugs was extracted. However beds and bedding were mentioned several times. It is possible that inventories for these estates would contain bed rugs.

The popularity of bed rugs accompanied American women westward after the Revolutionary War. In a will book for Caldwell County, Kentucky, Mary Smith gave her feather bed, bolster, two pillows, rug, bed stead etc. to a sister in 1831. In this same book Janett Mott left a will dated August 16, 1862 that bequeathed a red and white bed quilt. Ann M. Flournoy left a hexagon quilt and a Marseilles counterpane in a will dated September 21, 1869. Quilts and counterpanes remained popular bed covers in the 19th century. In seven wills probated between 1807 and 1811 in Franklin County, Kentucky no mention of rugs among other bedding was made. The wills did not mention any specific kinds of bedding only beds and furniture.

In a list of 182 inventories taken between May 7, 1811 and March 10, 1856 in Franklin County, Indiana, bed rugs were mentioned. In the inventory of Richard Minor made July 9, 1814 a bedstead, straw tick, sheet and old rug were listed. The inventories also referred to many other types of bed covers, particularly coverlets, quilts and counterpanes. A unique bed cover was noted in the inventory of Simpson Jones Jr. taken December 20, 1833. It listed a flowered bedspread. The value of this item is $2, and the value of a blue and white coverlet was listed at $2.50, a bird's eye coverlet at $1 and two calico quilts were valued at $3. This inventory appears in the Appendix. The inventory of the estate of Adam Nelson made September 10, 1819 included two rugs, but as the listing was not included with other bedding, these rugs could have been floor carpets. The use of carpeting on floors was becoming more popular. 19 out of the 182 inventories mentioned carpets.

Between April 23, 1833 and March 10, 1856, 44 inventories taken for estates in Ripley County, Indiana listed many textile items but no bed rugs. Bed covers that were listed included quilts, counterpanes and coverlets.

No bed rugs were mentioned in 53 inventories made between April 1, 1836 and November 5, 1859 in Dearborn County, Indiana. Other bedding mentioned included bedspreads and quilts. Carpeting was mentioned in six inventories. One of those inventories listed the items room by room and mentioned carpets in the sitting room, parlor, west room and hall. This inventory was for the estate of Abraham Roland taken on Oct. 8, 1859.

In an inventory made in 1843 of the estate of Peter Demory in Louden County, Virginia, a rug, listed after two lots of carpeting, may be interpreted as meaning a floor rug. By this time bed rugs were not as fashionable as other types of bed covers. Several instances of the mention of carpeting in wills at this time shows that carpets were not only a popular household accessory but also an important item; one important enough to be mentioned in a will.

The estate inventory of Elinor Pidcock of Mercer County, New Jersey, dated 1855, mentioned carpets in several rooms along with beds, bedsteads and furniture. As bed rugs were never called carpets it is safe to assume these were floor carpets. The house was filled with beds; no less than 12 beds were listed. Two and possibly three carpets were inventoried. One item, written 'caspet' could have been a carpet. Carpeting was also mentioned in an 1851 will in Greenbrier County, West Virginia. In the will of William Bradley of Sussex County, Delaware dated January 12, 1841, he wrote, "I give and bequeath to my beloved wife, Esther Bradley one bed, bedstead and furniture, one blue chest and one floor carpet extra of her dower, to her and her heirs forever." As late as 1888 wills in Delaware were still including beds and furniture.

Lost and Found

While a number of bed rugs have been found, others have been lost. Although many more bed rugs have been found than lost, the loss of even one bed rug makes an impact on the study of these covers, as there are so few extant rugs to begin with. The discovery of bed rugs has increased dramatically since the 1972 bed rug show at the Wadsworth Atheneum. That event sparked interest in the great shaggy bedspreads among many people, and taught others how to identify these items.

A dated 1782 bed rug with the initial 'A' and possibly a 'C' is among the list of missing bed rugs. It was pictured in *Antiques* magazine in 1929 and sold at an auction known as the Camp sale in January 1929.

This rug was a typical home-designed tree of life pattern with wandering vines holding floral motifs as it proceeded up each side of the rug. These vines were connected to a central bouquet composed of vines budding with floral motifs. The rug looks distorted because many of the colors have faded and have blended into the buff shades of the background. The darker sections are made with blue and black yarns. The color description was given by W. W. Kent in his book *The Hooked Rug* published in 1930 in which he described the rug as 'hooked'. He also stated the background of the rug was coarse linen but others have stated it was made of wool. The stitches of the rug were sheared to form a pile. Because of its similarity to many other tree of life design rugs found in New England, this rug was also attributed to that area of the country.

Another rug now lost was illustrated in several publications and was fashioned with sparse floral designs on thin vines flowing from a leafy base at the foot of the rug. There are three prominent floral motifs, one at each side at the foot of the rug and one in the upper part of the central section. Two hearts were placed at either side of the rug in the upper portion. Many small leaves completed the design. According to William L. Warren's research the flowers were white, blue, brown and yellow. He also wrote that the foundation material was wool upon which several strands of yarn were embroidered and the surface was left unsheared. The foot of the rug is curved and appears to have been made that way at the time of construction. The rug could have originated in the Connecticut River valley area of Massachusetts. It was owned at one time by the late Henry D. Sleeper of Boston and Gloucester, Mass. This rug also was illustrated in *The Hooked Rug* by W.W. Kent and identified as a hooked rug. The same bed cover was shown on the floor under a chest-on-chest in an advertisement in *Antiques* magazine in 1923.

One more lost rug is the one attributed to Melissa Hale, said to be a niece of Nathan Hale. This rug was pictured in the November 1913 issue of *House Beautiful* and was discussed earlier in a section on Hale family bed rugs.

Of more importance are the rugs that have been 'found'. Among those found is a wonderful example of a bed rug dated 1802 and bearing the initials, S F. The rug was sold at auction in 1989. It was described as 92 by 87 inches in size, worked with gold, rust, olive green and rose yarns and probably made in Connecticut. It would not be surprising to find that this rug was made by a member of the Foote family of Colchester. The reason for this is not only because of the similar last initial but because the design is similar to those made by the women of the Foote family. The rug is also similar to several other rugs including a rug made in 1796, initialed N L and now at the Metropolitan Museum of Art and to one at the Wadsworth Atheneum made in 1802 by Philena McCall of Lebanon, Connecticut.

The design is typical of many Connecticut bed rugs with the feathered-style vine rising out of a small leafy arrangement at the foot of the rug and winding around four carnation-like flowers on each side of the rug. Two more flowers are placed at the head and two at the foot of the rug. The central portion of the rug features a large floral bouquet of similar flowers held in place by one of the most popular motifs, the two-handled vase. Small flowers and leaves fill in the spaces between the larger motifs. This rug is so similar to many others in design if not coloring and stitch that is seems as if the makers must have had access to a pattern or a teacher's expertise, as there are at least nine others with this overall design.

Another rug that has been found was dated 1773. It is in remarkably good shape with vibrant colors. It must have been well cared for to survive 200 years in such good condition. The rug is very similar to a rug owned by the Currier Gallery in Manchester, New Hampshire. Both rugs have natural color background with trailing vines beginning at the base winding out of a large blue and yellow flower. Particularly notable are two large dissimilar flowers on each side of the cover embroidered in yellows and blues. The rug is a variant of the tree of life pattern. The central section contains three smaller yellow globe-like flowers with dark blue outer petals. Dark blue leaves are prominently embroidered on the outer edges of the rug. The rug has rounded corners at the foot of the spread that appear to have been a part of the original dimensions.

A rug with one side panel missing was offered at auction in 1984. Because bed rugs are so rare, even one with damage such as this one, is valuable. This rug was dated 1770 and contained the initials HH at the head of the cover. The rug was made with a rusty tan background with shades of green and blue flowers and vines. It contained a vine-like design starting at the foot of the rug under a leafy base and wound around floral motifs to the head of the bed in five vertical sections. The missing section of about 8 to 10 inches in width contained the majority of one of these vertical vine motifs.

Shelburne Museum received, as a gift, a bed rug that was made in 1819 by Dorothy (Harris) Seabury. She wrote her name and her husband, John's name, the date and the town 'Stow" at the head of the rug. The town of Stowe, Vermont was originally spelled Stow according to town records. The couple was married in October 1812. The rug was a gift to the museum from one of Mrs. Seabury's descendants.

The Seabury rug features seven large flowers embroidered with rounded petals and circular centers. Several smaller versions of this motif as well as several other style flowers were featured in the rug. The entire design rises from a jug-shaped vase at the center of the foot of the cover. An attractive tri-color zigzag border that frames the two sides and the curved bottom of the bed rug is reminiscent of several rugs made in the mid-18th century. The rug is 93 by 101 inches and is embroidered in shades of brown and gold on a black background. The large flowers are similar to the rug owned by the Antiquarian and Landmark Society of Connecticut.

A bed rug made by Esther Packard was brought to light at a New England auction in 1993. The maker signed her full name and the date 1801 to the rug that measures 82 by 86 inches. The colors used included red, cream, deep yellow, dark and light blue on a dark background. This rug is quite similar to a rug located at the Henry Ford Museum, Greenfield Village, Dearborn, Michigan, made by Rachel Packard of Jericho, Vermont. Her rug, initialed R P and dated 1805, was made when she was 71 years old. The bed cover, 93 ½-inches by 90 inches, is sewn with red, light blue, green, yellow and dark blue yarns on a black background embroidered with the running stitch. Both rugs have the central square motif at the center of the cover reminiscent of the earliest rugs dating back to the 1720-40 era such as the Hannah Baldwin rug dated 1741. The borders of the two rugs are similar tri-colored designs, one plain scallops and the other a combination of scallops and saw tooth motifs. A third rug similar to the two Packard rugs was advertised for sale in the early 1990's. It was signed with the initials R P and dated 1806. The owner attributes the rug to Rachel Packard, as it closely resembles the 1805 Rachel Packard rug. All three rugs contain a vine that loosely carries the floral motifs around the edge of the rug, and faint vine-like lines tie the central floral designs together.

Another rug that has been brought to light sold at an auction in 1996. In the embroidery it is signed Joseph and Olive Abbott, March 22, 1775. The bed cover features the typical tree of life pattern with vines running around the rug's edges holding flowers and bunches of grapes. The floral motifs are similar in pattern to many other bed rugs. It is finished with a scalloped border on the sides, but the foot of the rug appears to have been cut off, and the lower corners rounded at some later period. Vibrant colors were noted in the rug description at the time of the sale.

A rug found in Rhode Island is notable for the very fact that it survived harsh treatment. It was found in a thrift shop and at one time had been used as a floor rug under a small table. It appears that people were allowed to walk on the outer edges of the rug while it was used as a floor covering. As a result, the central section of the rug has survived but the outer edges are quite threadbare. The brown tones to the rug lend to its uniqueness. The floral design is similar to many of the bed rugs using the carnation-like floral motifs in both the central section and the outer edges. The colors used include browns, greens, and rust shades and natural background. The stitch is the cut loop pile running stitch. It is located at the University of Rhode Island textile collection.

Other 'found' rugs include the Lorraine Collins rug and the Patience Foote rug both described elsewhere in this book. There was one example of a bed rug that was found in such a deplorable condition that the owner threw it away, and there are probably others that have come to light but not to my attention.

The Welsh Bed Rugs

Several bed rugs are located at the National Museum of Wales, in the Welsh Folk Museum, located in St. Fagan's near Cardiff.

The Welsh rugs are the common type, the single-colored bed rug, that was often imported from Europe and Britain to this country in the 17th and 18th century. Advertisements in Boston and New York newspapers attest to their availability at this time. For example an advertisement in the *Boston Gazette* printed on Sept. 1, 1760 offered bed rugs, counterpanes, floor carpets and red check fabric for bed curtains. Spotted rugs and quarter rugs also appeared in advertisements of Boston merchants.

The Welsh rugs are of natural color wool and are made with a knotted pile. The construction consists of an underlying woolen foundation of about 18 ends per inch in both warp and weft. The weave is a plain weave.

Knots were made with seven strands of yarn. The one-third inch knots were set in the background horizontally at regular intervals across the fabric. Approximately six rows of the background fabric lie in between each row of knots. The knots were made on a previously woven piece of cloth. The rug is approximately 36 by 72 inches, single bed size.

The provenance for this cover is a village near St. Fagan's, west of Cardiff. Two other covers at the museum are similar in style and color. One came from Penuwch in Ceredigion, Dyfed in West Wales and the other was from Dolgellau, Gwynedd in Northwest Wales.

The Welsh Folk Museum was founded in 1947, when the castle and land were donated by the Earl of Plymouth to the National Museum of Wales as a center for a folk museum. The castle, built in 1580, has been restored to its 17th century appearance. The grounds surrounding the castle contain a recreated folk village with a school, shops, mill, cottages, farmhouses and barns.

Bed rugs are not commonly found now in Britain or Europe. An inquiry about bed rugs in England was made in 1996 to the Victoria and Albert Museum in London and their reply was that they knew of no bed rugs in their collection. The letter stated that bed rugs are not as cherished in Britain as they are in America and so tend not to survive. It must also be remembered that Britain was involved in two world wars in the 20th century and great shortages of almost everything occurred. Many stored items, such as old bedding would be put back in use and worn out before the wars were ended.

A single color rug is now in the collection of Winterthur Museum in Delaware. It is constructed with a tufted stitch of woolen yarn knotted onto a linen background and then piece-dyed a dark green. It was probably made in Britain or Europe.

The Norsk Folkemuseum near Oslo, Norway and the Hauseatiske Museum in Bergen, Norway both have a type of bed rug, called ryijys, in their collections. They are constructed by the knotted stitch method done either as the weaving progressed or after the foundation fabric was removed from the loom.

Bed rugs were found mentioned in English farm and cottage inventories and they were also mentioned at the estate of Knole in 1624. Documents at this estate refer to a white rug for a bed that had crimson and white taffeta curtains and a valance of white satin embroidered with crimson and white silk with a deep matching fringe. In the 1663 will of an Englishman from Chelmsford one of his best white rugs was bequeathed to one person and his worst white rug to another.

Early records show that colonists brought rugs to the New World. Persons planning to go to Maryland were advised by Lord Baltimore to bring rugs with them, and John Winthrop brought rugs on his voyage to America in March 1630. Winthrop wrote upon his arrival in New England, to his son John, who had remained in England, to bring more rugs to use and to sell. The imported rug was never described as colorful or floral or of an intricate geometric pattern. The description of imported rugs refers mostly to their source, such as Irish, Polish, Bilbao, Biscay or English. Most rugs imported to America were from Ireland or England. Descriptive phrases referring to rugs were limited to plain, striped or spotted.

Compass Rose Blankets

Embroidered compass rose blankets were fashioned from plain woolen blankets, mostly of natural color wool, by embroidering a polychrome circular design of approximately 15 inches in diameter in each corner of the blanket. The design resembled the decorative compass-like design found on early maps. The most inexperienced needleworker could make this simple design, and many were probably fashioned by young girls as a beginner's needlework project. It was an inexpensive way to brighten up an otherwise Spartan bedchamber.

Most entries in probate inventories that refer to a rose blanket probably mean the embroidered compass rose blanket, as a rose-colored blanket was a scarce item. Solid color blankets were most often natural. Other colors inventoried included blue, mustard, yellow and dull green. One example is the rose blanket mentioned in the estate inventory of Jesse Cook of Coventry, Connecticut taken July 3, 1792. Listed was a "blue rose coverlid" valued at 18 shillings. A second rose coverlet was valued at 12 shillings. Also in this inventory is the intriguing listing of one figured coverlet at 15 shillings and a blue and yellow coverlet at five shillings. These might have been overshot woven coverlets as the Cook inventory listed a handloom and fabric by the yard.

In this same year George Washington ordered rose blankets among other bedding, to furnish the new executive mansion in Philadelphia, Pennsylvania.

The estate inventory of Judith Carter of Hebron, Connecticut entered into probate August 7, 1792 listed a variety of bedding including a compass worked bed quilt valued at 15 shillings.

When the word 'worked' was mentioned in listing textiles, it most often meant that the item had been embroidered. The reference to this embroidered item as a quilt probably meant it was used as a bed spread covering the other bedding. This compass embroidered quilt was more highly valued than her bed rug that was valued at four shillings, six pence.

In the inventory of Col. Joel Jones of Hebron, Connecticut taken Aug. 29, 1792 one compass worked coverlet was listed among his other bedding. The reference to the blanket as a coverlet probably meant it was used as a top covering or bedspread on one of the home's bedsteads. The value of this item was 20 shillings. It was given a higher value than a bed quilt partly made of baize wool and also higher than rag coverlets. The inventory also included another compass worked coverlet valued at five shillings.

Rose blankets were listed in the estate inventory of Richard Hale Jr. of Coventry, Connecticut, who died in 1793. He was a brother of Nathan Hale, the martyr-spy of the American Revolutionary War. The estate inventory of David Hale of Coventry, also a brother of Nathan Hale, taken in 1822, listed four rose blankets. They were valued approximately the same as quilts and plaid blankets in the inventory. This could be interpreted as meaning they were of equal value or possibly more worn than the other items. Some inventory takers listed the condition of items in the inventories but the condition of the textiles in David Hale's inventory was not noted.

The estate of Nathan Hale's sister, Elizabeth (Hale) Taylor of Coventry, who died in 1813, listed one large rose blanket and one small rose blanket among other blankets and coverlets that were described by color, including white, purple and white, as well as just light and dark blankets. No mention of embroidery or worked items was made in the inventory.

In the inventory of the estate of John Post of Hebron, Connecticut in 1844 a rose blanket was listed as well as a worked counterpane. This last item could have been an embroidered bedspread done with woolen yarns more commonly known today as a crewel bedspread, or it could have been a bed rug. It was valued at four dollars.

Other Embroidered Bed Covers

Embroidered bed covers were a very popular form of needlework in 18th and early 19th century America. They were made at the same time as women were making bed rugs and continued to be made several decades after women ceased to make bed rugs.

The main difference between the two covers is that the stitchery on the embroidered wool on wool or wool on linen cover did not entirely cover the background fabric. Harriet or Hannah Dunbar of Lenox, Massachusetts embroidered a wool on wool cover in 1760 with a design that was similar to bed rug designs but stitched with finer yarns. The colors of the two-ply, crewel-type embroidery yarn were peach, red, rose, yellow, olive green, light blue and light brown with an olive green fringe worked on a dark blue woolen blanket. All the stitches were done with this fine yarn except the centers of the large flowers and these were worked with multi-plied yarn in the running stitch, the stitch common to many bed rugs. This type of bed cover, referred to today as a crewel bedspread, was known originally as a worked cover. The word crewel comes from the type of yarn used for embroidery and has been transposed since that time to refer to embroidered fabrics.

Another embroidered coverlet using a checked, twill weave woolen blanket for a foundation made use of the woven pattern of white bars on dark blue ground as a basis for the embroidery pattern. Each square formed by the woven check contained four similar embroidered elements. The outer squares of the bed cover contain floral designs held together by a serpentine vine that winds around the sides and foot of the cover. The embroidery, made with white yarn, was executed in the running stitch with cut pile and chain stitch.

A wool on wool embroidered blanket is on display in the second floor schoolroom chamber at Nathan Hale Homestead, Coventry, Connecticut. It is approximately 77 by 85 inches in a twill weave. This cover is woven of white wool with a dark blue plaid pattern that created a pattern of 6½-inch white squares into which the needle worker stitched a solid dark blue floral motif. There are 11 white blocks across the width of the blanket and 12 blocks vertically from head to foot. To create the plaid pattern the weaver used two blue threads separated from each other by eight white threads. Each blue stripe contained four threads repeated at 6½-inch intervals. The plaid pattern is formed by squaring the design in the weaving. The pattern was embroidered in dark blue yarn, using the laid stitch, a filling stitch used in the past by many frugal New England women. This stitch leaves most of the embroidery on the surface of the foundation fabric. The stitch is also referred to as the New England laid stitch or Roumanian couching stitch.

The embroidery made with this stitch covers areas solidly but the surface of the embroidery does not have the smooth effect that is made by the use of the satin stitch. A small stitch in the center of each vertical row of stitches is twisted and although it covers the area economically it is not smooth. The effect from a distance however is similar to the less economical satin stitch that used as much yarn on the back as on the surface of the material. A single strand of yarn was used in the embroidery.

The pattern made with the laid stitch was a 3½-inch diameter eight-pointed flower from which a graceful curved stem and tiny leaf trailed. This flower was carefully duplicated in each white square all over the blanket. A white woolen, knotted fringe on the sides and foot of the cover that was made with two-ply yarn completed the project. The initials O and M separated by a half-size X, placed at the head of the blanket, were embroidered in cross stitching using the same dark blue yarn. The O and M are probably initials and the X might have been the Roman numeral for 10. Sheets and blankets were often numbered.

A similar cover, in the author's collection, featured a dark blue plaid pattern on a white background made of linen. It was embroidered in dark blue wool in each white square created by the woven plaid design. The embroidery pattern consists of four-lobed floral motifs stitched in each white square. In half of these designs is a single round dark blue center and the remaining motifs contain similar centers plus round dark blue circles in each lobe. The bedspread measures 76 inches square and was made of two widths of fabric stitched at the center. The fabric has 26 ends of linen yarn per inch in the warp and 18 rows of linen yarn per inch of weft.

Many embroidered bed covers made in America on linen foundations were artistically fanciful and intricate. Floral designs were the most popular motif. They were similar to embroidered bed covers made in England but American women used crewel yarns more sparingly and the motifs were sparser than their European counterparts.

One of the most elaborate bed cover and matching hangings known today were made by Mary (Swett) Bulman about 1745. They are on display at the Emerson-Wilcox House in York, Maine, a gift to the museum by a descendant of the maker. The set is filled with colorful large floral designs held together with intricate vines interspersed with flowers and fruit. The valence is filled with floral designs and quotations of poetry running around the entire piece. The poetry she embroidered is from Isaac Watt's "Meditation in a Grove" from his *Horae Lyricae* (1706). This is one of the best-preserved and most complete sets of bed furnishings of American origin.

It is believed that Mary Bulman made the embroidered hangings and spread at the time her husband, Dr. Alexander Bulman, left for Canada, circa 1745. Dr Bulman served as a surgeon with the British and American fighting forces during the attack against the French held Fort Louisbourg, Cape Breton, Nova Scotia. A native of Kittery, Maine, Dr. Bulman died at Fort Louisbourg.

It is not known where Mary Bulman learned the art of embroidery but it is evident that she was well educated not only in embroidery but in literature as well. Her artistically placed motifs are enhanced with her use of color throughout the bed furnishings, and the careful embroidery of poetry stitched on the valence is remarkable. Several of the motifs in the central section of the head cloth are very similar to motifs used in bed rugs, in particular the floral bouquets emanating from vases.

Several years after the doctor's death, Mary Bulman married the Rev. Thomas Prentice of Charlestown, Massachusetts. In 1778, after she was again widowed, Mary

Bulman Prentice returned to York, where she died. She is buried in York's Old Burying Ground near the museum where her embroidery is displayed.

The earliest quilts found in America were made of wool or silk. Most early quilts were imported. Woolen whole cloth quilts, usually of a solid color were often intricately embellished with attractively patterned designs stitched with the simple quilting stitch, a fine running stitch using a thread dyed to match the foundation fabric. Some of these quilting patterns are similar to motifs used to make bed rugs.

These quilts, known as whole cloth quilts, calamanco or linsey-woolsey, were made larger than other bed covers probably because they often were the uppermost cover on a bed and needed to be large to cover a multitude of winter blankets. Most of these quilts were made in dark blue, but red, pink, light blue, green, mustard and brown whole cloth quilts have also survived. Many of these quilts have a glazed surface.

The word calamanco is derived from the phrase, glazed camlet. This type of fabric was also used for clothing in the 18th century in America and in Europe. Linsey-woolsey quilts were woven with a combination of woolen and linen yarns.

Needle workers used cotton foundations for embroidered bed covers when that fabric became more readily available in the early 19th century. These were generally done on white cotton and are referred to as white on white or white work bedspreads. This craft increased in popularity in America at the end of the Revolutionary War and became very fashionable in the early 19th century. The white on white factory-made bedspreads woven in Bolton, England were copied by many Americans who could not afford the purchased spread. By making their own bedspreads, they fashioned covers with lasting appeal by using their names, initials and dates along with their favorite American motifs. Many variations of white work were made and all required a great deal of skill, not only because of the intricate stitches, but because it was difficult to follow the pattern with an all white project.

Some of the white work patterns resemble the bed rug designs, including the large central motif that often included a vase with a bouquet of flowers, surrounded by trailing vines and floral designs. The bed rug running loop-pile stitch combined with several other stitches to fashion the bedspread was often found in the white bedspreads. When used in this type of bedding the loop-pile stitch was usually cut.

Other techniques used to make white on white bedspreads were corded, stuffed, all-over quilting, and candlewicking. By the time these white on white covers were at the height of their popularity it appears that bed rug making was at an end. Like all popular fashions, whether it was architecture, home furnishings or costume, styles were slower to become outdated in the rural, country areas because new styles were slower to reach those areas. Because bed rugs were made generally in rural areas they would have been made for a longer period of time than they would have if they had been used to furnish town houses.

Even though the bed rug eventually declined in popularity, the bed rug idea did not suddenly disappear. It evolved into small carpets used as hearth rugs, as stair carpets, and occasionally the loop-pile stitch, that was used to make bed rugs, was placed on upholstered footstools.

.

The Art of Making a Bed Rug

Skills in hand weaving, hand spinning, natural dyeing and surface design embroidery are needed to construct a bed rug. To make an exact replica bed rug, enough yarn should be spun to weave a blanket for the background foundation. Women in the 18th century used a singles hand spun yarn to weave their blankets. Approximately 11,000 yards would be needed to weave the blanket that has 18 ends per inch in both the warp and weft. A better fabric is made if the Z-spun warp yarns are combined with S-spun weft yarns. A similar type of factory-made weaving yarn can be purchased from hand weaving suppliers. The warp should be set 45 or more inches wide on the loom and seven yards long to allow for loom take-up. When taken from the loom the fabric should be gently washed and air-dried so that it does not shrink or felt. This fabric would then be cut and stitched together to create a blanket with a center seam and hemmed at the top and bottom. The blanket then would be approximately 86 by 108 inches.

Another option for the craftsman would be to purchase an antique woolen blanket or linen sheet. Antique hand-woven bedding varies in size and condition, two important factors to consider before purchase of antique fabrics.

A third option would be to purchase enough woolen or linen fabric to use for a bed rug foundation. A plain weave woolen or even weave linen fabric is best, but a twill weave woolen or linen foundation could be used for the types of bed rugs that do not employ the embroidered darning stitch technique.

In order to calculate the yardage needed for handspun yarn for the embroidery, test samples should be made using the various stitches to be employed in the rug. It is easiest to calculate the plain background yardage but multicolor floral designs will have to be estimated. To calculate yardage, stitch a square inch of embroidery with pre-measured lengths of yarn. Make several samples to get an accurate measurement. The embroidery yarn could also be purchased from hand weaving suppliers. The same yarn used for weaving could be used for the embroidery. Most bed rugs are not embroidered with plied yarn but with several strands of single ply yarn.

Use a blunt needle to make the stitches so that the needle does not damage the foundation fabric. The size of the needle's eye depends on the number of strands and weight of the yarn to be used. Less damage is done to the foundation fabric with small-eye needles. Hoops need not be used but might be helpful in the darning stitch embroidery technique, where careful attention is needed to count the warp and weft threads of the background fabric. The embroidery yarn is fragile and short lengths of yarn are used so it does not fray and break. The most important feature of a bed rug is that the embroidery must cover the entire surface of the background.

Three to five strands of yarn were used in the 1771 bed rug made in Coventry, Connecticut by Esther Lyman. Four strands of yarn were used to make the knots in the bed rug that is now at the Daughters of the American Revolution Headquarters in Norwich, Connecticut.

The maker of one of the rugs now at Historic Deerfield, Deerfield, Massachusetts used two to five strands of dyed wool yarn in the patterns of her bed cover and eight strands of unbleached wool yarn in the background area of this rug. The rug was made with darning stitches and running stitches.

The finer the yarn the more strands should be used in the needle. Some bed rug makers used worsted yarns to stitch their rugs, or a combination of worsted and woolen yarns. Worsted is usually a smoother yarn and often has more sheen than woolen yarn. The difference in the two yarns is due to the type of sheep from which the fleece is obtained and to the way the wool was prepared for spinning. Woolen fibers are carded and worsted fibers are combed. The hand spinning process is similar for both types of yarn.

A variety of stitches and knots were used to make bed rugs. They were: the running loop pile stitch, which was the most common stitch found in bed rugs; the darning stitch; the stem stitch, a type of back stitch; and the double stitched pile as found in a bed rug now in New Brunswick, Canada.

Another technique used to make bed rugs was knotted pile. This was done either when the fabric was being woven or after the fabric was taken from the loom. Rows of knots were made in the foundation separated by several rows of plain background, which would be covered by the shaggy effect of the knots. This technique is similar to the ryijy rugs found in Scandinavia.

Using a uniform length running stitch and leaving the embroidery yarn looped on the surface of each stitch makes the common loop pile running stitch. A loop measure that is sometimes employed by rug makers is not necessary for this type of stitch. The needle worker will create an even pile through practice. Some rug makers left the loops uncut, others cut all the loops and still others cut loops in certain areas only. Some antique rugs have been clipped in recent years in an effort to 'renew' the surface of the rug.

The darning stitches require a finer smoother yarn, and worsted yarns were favored over woolen yarn for this stitch. Fewer strands of the yarn were used in the needle compared with the amounts used in the loop pile stitchery. The stem stitch, that was used to make one bed rug, is also known as the crewel stitch. Other stitches that could be used include the double stitched pile and the darning stitch.

The designs for bed rugs are large and bold with few details. It is best to remember that the rug will be viewed most often on the bed so the most important parts of the rug are the central section at the foot of the spread, the center section of the bed, and the area that rises up over the pillows. Large flowers and leaves that were held together with vines were popular motifs on bed rugs. Most rugs contain three to five large flowers along each lengthwise edge of the rug. Large designs were often placed at the foot, in the center and at the head of the rug. Many bed rug makers used a two-handled vase at the foot of the rug from which vines holding the floral and leaf arrangements rose and meandered around the rug, in a loose design. Strong central features used by bed rug makers include a large sunburst design; a single large flower and some bed rug makers used the double-handled vase in the center portion of the rug. The vase held a spray of flowers. When the vase was in the center of the rug, a leaf motif or another vase design was placed at the foot of the rug to hold the vines that trailed around the outside of the rug.

Most bed rugs have a vine-like pattern that holds the rug together, and floral motifs and leaves are tied to the vines. In some rugs these vines are more prominent and wider and in other rugs they are only one stitch wide. Even the smaller incidental flowers and leaves, fruits and birds are all connected to this vine pattern creating the effect of a giant bouquet.

Some bed rugs had special places designed in the pattern for the inclusion of dates, initials or whole names. Other bed rug makers added the initials and dates as an afterthought. Most bed rug makers placed the identifying initials at the head of the rug and one rug maker, Mary Comstock, stitched her name and the date 1810 so large that it took up nearly one quarter of the rug. This rug was discussed in an earlier chapter. New bed rugs should always include at least initials and dates. If a bed rug is to be made using the woven technique, the initials or names and date can be embroidered on the rug upon completion. Complete identification of the maker can be placed on a linen tape and sewn to the underside of a new bed rug.

Many rugs had similar designs and may have been copied from one needle worker to another. Other possibilities are that paper patterns might have been exchanged or designs were purchased from teachers. Some women would be artistic enough to copy a neighbor's bed rug from memory, or include some motifs from her neighbor's rug and some of her own invention.

Paper, though scarce in the 18th and early 19th century was available from many merchants in the larger towns. Caleb Davis listed choice press paper at his paper mill for two guineas per gross in the Feb. 18, 1765 *Boston Gazette* advertisement. Imported paper was available in 1763 from John Perkins at his Boston stationery shop, according to an advertisement in the *Boston Gazette*. Needle workers also used fine linen, cotton or silk fabric to draw patterns for embroidery.

A paper pattern for a bed rug drawn by Olive Curtiss is in the collection of Pocumtuck Valley Memorial Association, Deerfield, Massachusetts. She lived in Durham, Connecticut and moved to Granville, Massachusetts after her marriage to the Rev. Joel Baker. Written on the back of the pattern is Olive Curtiss' name and the date 1798. The bed rug, if it was ever made, has not been found.

The design for a new bed rug should be drawn on paper and then enlarged to proper size when the plan is completed. The enlargement may be made by using the graph method. For example choose a flower that is four inches square and needs to be 16 inches square. Draw one-inch square cross hatching all over the pattern, and then on a separate piece of paper draw at least four, four-inch squares of cross-hatching.

Copy the design from the small graph to the large graph by drawing in each of the large squares the design that appears in the corresponding one-inch square of the original pattern. When the design has been transferred to the new sheet it will be four times larger than the original. To make a specific design to a larger size, copy the original design on tracing paper and rule the tracing into one-inch size squares. Calculate the desired size needed and mark this size on another piece of tracing paper. Divide the larger number by the smaller number of squares and the resulting number is the size in inches of the full-size pattern. For example, when a pattern is five inches across, but a 15" pattern is desired, then the size of the squares for the new pattern should be three inches. See illustration on page 77 for enlarging patterns.

Applying the design to the background fabric can be accomplished in several ways. One method is to make full-size patterns on stiff paper, cut out the patterns and draw around them onto the background with a water-soluble pencil or ink. Another method is to use a paper pattern with the design lines pricked with a pounce wheel, then sifting dark powder, such as charcoal or powdered colored chalk through the holes onto the fabric. The dusty outline is then drawn over with water-soluble pencil or ink. This was a method used by Michelangelo to put patterns for his painted scenes on the end wall and ceiling of the Sistine Chapel.

Women in the 18th and 19th century made water-soluble ink by using the blue paper in which white, cone sugar was wrapped. The paper was soaked in a small amount of water to extract the blue coloring and this was used as ink for pattern making. The blue wrappers kept the sugar cones white and clean during shipping and storage. Imported cochineal dye also was used as ink. When used without a mordant this dye is water-soluble. Miss Lambert wrote a recipe for ink in her 1843 book *The Handbook of Needlework* using indigo dissolved in spirits of wine with small, equal amounts of gum Arabic and sugar. Iron-on transfers were not used until 1875. One other effective way of copying designs is to trace the pattern onto a second sheet of paper by holding the pattern and paper up to the light at a window. Another method is to use carbon paper or dressmaker's carbon paper to transfer designs from paper pattern to foundation fabric. In the 19th century Dr. A.W. Chase gave a recipe for making carbon paper that was so simple that it could have been used in much earlier years. The recipe is for *Magic Paper - Used to Transfer Figures in Embroidery, or Impressions for Herbariums*. "Take lard-oil, or sweet-oil, mixed to the consistence of cream with either of the following paints, the color of which is desired: Prussian blue, lamp-black, Venetian red or chrome green, either of which should be rubbed, with a knife on a plate or stone until smooth. Use rather thin, but firm paper; put on with a sponge and wipe off as dry as convenient; then lay them between uncolored paper, or between newspapers, and press by laying books or some other flat substance upon them, until the surplus oil is absorbed, when it is ready for use. Directions - For taking off patterns of embroidery place a piece of thin paper over the embroidery to prevent soiling; then lay on the magic paper, and put on the cloth you wish to take the copy on, to embroider; pin fast and rub over with a spoon handle; and every part of the raised figure will show up on the plain cloth." This recipe was included in the 27th edition of *Dr. Chase's Recipes* published in 1866.

Once the foundation fabric is determined, the embroidery yarn spun or purchased, the pattern designed and placed on the background, the natural dying can begin. Colors most often found in bed rugs were blue and brown, with undyed natural color yarn. Other colors used were red, yellow, buff, tan, gray, orange, green, black and purple.

Natural dyes used to make these colors came from indigo for blues, madder for reds and fustic for tans and yellows. Logwood, weld, woad, cutch and cochineal were also available from merchants. Purchased dyes were augmented by native American plants, especially walnut hulls for brown, oak and maple bark for buff, gold or orange.

Native plants require a great amount of material to give good color to the dye bath, so items easily gathered such as bark, nut hulls or goldenrod would have been used more frequently than coreopsis blossoms and lily of the valley leaves.

Purchased imported dyes were available in many towns. The Ewing & Barns establishment in Somers, Connecticut advertised on Monday, Feb. 19, 1787 in the *Connecticut Courant and Weekly Intelligencer,* many household items including the dyes copperas, logwood and indigo. Their other wares included fabrics, sewing notions, hardware, cookware, books, coffee, tea, rum and spices. This paper was published in Hartford, Connecticut by Hudson & Goodwin Co.

The store of Joseph Lynde in Hartford Connecticut, advertised drugs and medicines, but he also carried spices, sugar and other imported food, crockery, glassware, paints, and dyes including fustic, madder, annatto, copperas and oil of vitriol. His ad ran in the *Connecticut Courant and Weekly Intelligencer* on Monday Oct. 22, 1787.

Twenty-five years later an advertisement appeared in the Hartford newspaper for Daniel Hopkins' wholesale and retail dye store. He advertised his wares on Tuesday, Aug. 10, 1812 in the same newspaper, known by that time as the *Connecticut Courant,* printed by Hudson and Goodwin. Hopkins listed for sale the following dyes: campeachy and St. Domingo logwood, fustic, camwood, English copperas, alum, nut galls, redwood, blue vitriol, madder, verdigris, argol or crude tartar, cream of tartar, borax, grain tin, turmeric, cochineal, annatto, safflowers, cudbear, and indigo from Spain, Bengal, Guatemala, Isle of France, and New Orleans.

It was possible in early America for women to hire other women to spin and weave. It was recorded in the *Vermont Gazetteer* in 1803 that Electa Marshall at the age of 12 worked out spinning tow (coarse linen yarn) at 42 cents a week. Both Abigail and Elizabeth Foote of Colchester mentioned in their diaries of being employed by others to card and spin. It was also possible to buy purchased indigo dyed yarn and fabric. According to an advertisement in the *Connecticut Courant* published in Hartford, on Sept. 29, 1812, Matthew Laflin and Son Co. of Southwick, Massachusetts stated they would execute blue dyeing at their establishment "in all its various branches." Several other companies advertised in the *Courant* custom dyeing and other textile work such as carding fleeces and weaving, fulling and dressing of fabric.

When the all the motifs have been embroidered and the background completely filled in with stitches, the rug is nearly complete. To finish the rug, make a simple knotted fringe around the two sides and foot of the rug, using the background color or a combination of any of the colors used in the rug. This covers the hemmed edges at the foot of the rug and the selvedges at the sides of the rug. Not all of the old bed rugs have fringe now. Some probably never had fringe, others have lost the fringe through wear and some rugs have only small amounts of fringe left here and there.

DYE RECIPES

Almost every family had dye recipes for coloring wool and linen yarns and many were passed on orally, from mother to daughter. A few were recorded on paper. The dye recipes included here are for their historical nature and not intended as instructions to be used to make natural dyes. Many modern natural dye books contain up-to-date recipes for natural dyeing.

Slate Dye with Beech Bark

Boil beech bark chips in an iron kettle until the color is imparted into the water, then skim out the chips and add copperas to set the dye. One pound of dried beech bark will dye one pound of woolen yarn. For a darker shade add more copperas but be careful as too much copperas makes the yarn brittle.

Yellow for Wool with Fustic

For each pound of wool yarn add three ounces of alum, one ounce of cream of tartar and one pound of fustic chips to four gallons of scalding hot water in a brass or copper kettle. Enter the wool yarn and bring the dye pot to a boil and boil for one and one-half hours. Take the yarn out cool it and gently rinse. Empty out the kettle and add four gallons of water. Place in a thin cloth bag one pound of fustic that has been cut up fine. Enter the fustic into the water and boil this mixture for two hours. Take out the fustic bag and enter the yarn and stir while boiling for one hour before taking out to cool and then rinse the yarn. Hickory or yellow oak bark can be used if fustic, a purchased dye, cannot be obtained. Fustic is a species of mulberry tree that grows in the West Indies and South America. It was used to make yellow, drab, olive and green dye.

Indigo for Blue Dye

Indigo, the most important dye plant before the advent of chemical dyes, is produced from the leaves of the plant *indigofera*. It was raised in South America, the East

Indies, India, Central America and other warm areas including the southern colonies in America. There were varying qualities of indigo and the best type was thought to be from India followed by that imported from Guatemala. Tests to ascertain the quality of indigo were made by women before they started dyeing. One of these tests was to set the cake of dried indigo into a bucket of water. The best indigo would float and the deeper the cake sank, the more impurities the cake contained. The color of the cake should be a deep blue and when rubbed with a fingernail a copper hue should appear.

To color three pounds of wool put one pail of chamberlye into a clean tub then dissolve two ounces of potash (substance obtained from leaching wood ashes) or three ounces of pearlash, (potassium carbonate) in two cups of hot water. Let the mixture stand for six days then pour off the clear part into another kettle being careful not to add the settlings into the kettle with the clear liquid. Throw the settlings away and rinse this kettle well. Pour the clear liquid back into this kettle.

The next procedure is to take 2 ounces of indigo and 1 ounce of madder and place them in a thin cloth bag and enter into the dye kettle stirring well four or five times during the day. Then enter the wool and leave it immersed for six hours, take it out and air it. The yarn turns blue when it is exposed to the air. If the yarn is not dark enough, reenter the wool in the dye vat and let it remain several more hours, then take it out and air it to check on the depth of color. The dye vat was not placed on the fire, but was kept in a warm place, near fire in cooler months and in a warm place out doors in summer. The quality of indigo will greatly affect the color of the yarn. If the indigo has a lot of impurities, or is from an inferior plant, the blue will not be as intense as with a good quality indigo.

Red Dye with Madder

For each pound of wool yarn to be dyed place 5 ounces of alum, one ounce of cream of tartar into a kettle of hot water, place the wet yarn into the kettle and simmer for one-half hour. Take out the yarn and air then simmer one-half hour longer. Empty the kettle and fill with clean water, add one peck of bran and heat until the mixture is lukewarm. Let the kettle stand until the bran rises, then skim off the bran and put in one-half pound of madder and then enter the yarn and heat slowly until it boils and the shade of red desired is achieved. Remove yarn and cool then rinse in soapy water until the rinse water is clear. Hang yarn in the shade to dry, moving frequently to dry evenly. Madder is a plant native to warm countries. The plants are raised for several years before the plant roots are harvested and dried. The roots should be chopped fine before using.

Layouts of Various Bed Rugs

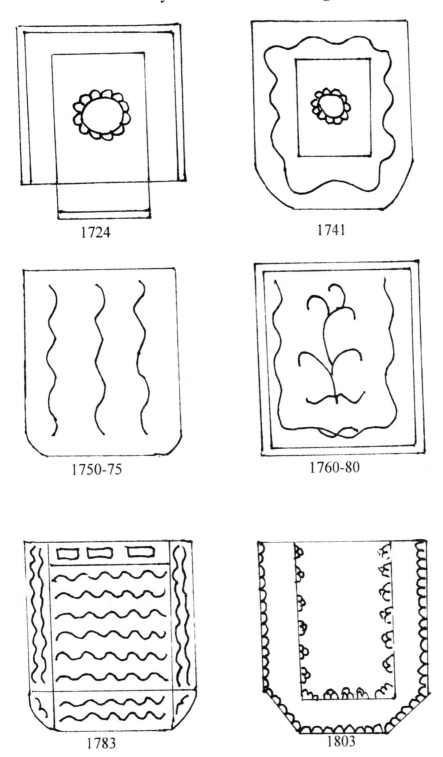

1724

1741

1750-75

1760-80

1783

1803

69

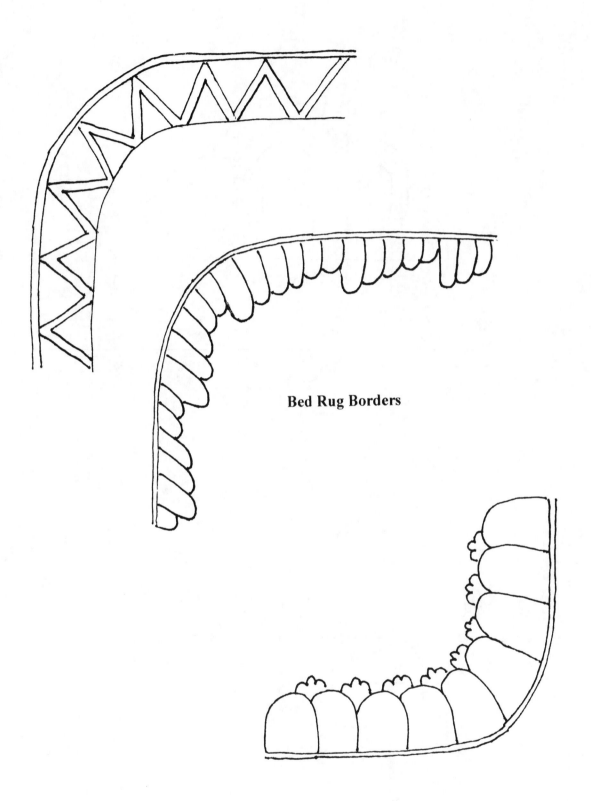

Bed Rug Borders

76

To Enlarge a Motif

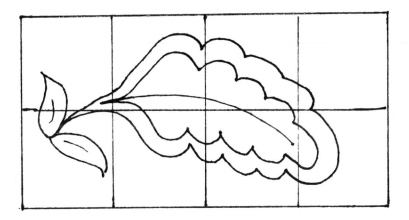

To enlarge this motif three times, increase the size
of each square from one inch to three inches.

Locations of Bed Rugs

Addison Gallery of American Art, Phillips Academy — Andover, Massachusetts

American Museum in Britain, Claverton Manor — Bath, England

Antiquarian and Landmarks Society of Connecticut, Inc. — Hartford, Connecticut

Art Institute of Chicago — Chicago, Illinois

Brooklyn Museum — Brooklyn, New York

Colonial Williamsburg Foundation — Williamsburg, Virginia

Connecticut Historical Society — Hartford, Connecticut

Currier Gallery of Art — Manchester, New Hampshire

Faith Trumbull Chapter, Connecticut Daughters of the American Revolution — Norwich, Connecticut

Governor Jonathan Trumbull House, Connecticut Daughters of the American Revolution — Lebanon, Connecticut

Greenfield Village and Henry Ford Museum — Dearborn, Michigan

Henry Francis du Pont Winterthur Museum — Winterthur, Delaware

Historic Deerfield Inc. — Deerfield, Massachusetts

Metropolitan Museum — New York, New York

Museum of Early Southern Decorative Arts	Winston-Salem, North Carolina
Museum of the Daughters of the American Revolution	Washington, D.C.
National Museum of Wales	St. Fagan's, Cardiff, Wales
New Brunswick Museum	St. John, New Brunswick, Canada
New York State Historical Association	Cooperstown, New York
New York Historical Society	New York, New York
Old York Historical Society	York, Maine
Peabody Essex Museum	Salem, Massachusetts
Shelburne Museum	Shelburne, Vermont
Smithsonian National Museum of History and Technology	Washington, D.C.
The Society for the Preservation of New England Antiquities	Boston, Massachusetts
Wenham Historical Association and Museum	Wenham, Massachusetts
Yale University Art Gallery	New Haven, Connecticut

Glossary

Baize – a heavy, felted, woolen cloth usually napped or raised on both sides.

Bed furnishings – the bed curtains, head cloth, valences, tester and bed cover.

Bedstead – the frame of the bed.

Blanket – a woolen fabric used for bed covers, most often natural color, either twill or plain weave, and sometimes woven with a colored stripe of blue, red, brown or black at each end. They were imported from England and made in America.

Bolton Coverlet – made in Bolton, near Manchester, England, called a counterpane, and woven of cotton with a looped-pile technique in the early 19th century. Hand embroidered cotton coverlets were made in America to imitate Bolton coverlets.

Boutonne – a weft-loop weave found in Bolton coverlets. Canadian weavers who used colored wools or heavy cotton to create the raised surface design also used this technique.

Calamanco – a plain weave, glazed worsted textile in solid colors including light blue, deep indigo, green, red and pink, often erroneously referred to as linsey-woolsey. The fabric was used as bedding and for clothing. In George F. Dow's book, *Arts and Crafts of New England*, on page 157, he referred to an advertisement in the Boston Gazette in 1737 listing "striped and plain calamancoes."

Check – a fabric made of any fibers with colored warp and weft stripes intersecting at right angles to form squares. Intricately checked fabrics are referred to as plaids.

Cochineal – a red dye made from the dried bodies of the insect cochina. This dye was also used as food coloring and in cosmetics.

Crewel – a loosely twisted, fine, two-ply worsted yarn made especially for embroidery. Dow quotes from the *Boston Gazette* on Oct. 15, 1751 on page 162, "Shades of Floss, Crewills & fine Silk ..."

Darning stitch – used in embroidery is a running stitch where the greater amount of yarn was left on the surface of the foundation fabric and smaller amount under the surface.

Fustic – a yellow dye from the tree *Chlorophora tinctora.*

Indigo – a dye obtained from the plant *Indigofera tinctora*, native to India but also grown in Spain, Guatemala and other warm countries.

Ingrain carpet – a heavy, double-cloth fabric of several colors that is interwoven. The yard-wide strips of carpeting were sewn together for room-size carpeting. Also referred to as Scotch carpets.

Linsey-Woolsey – a coarse cloth made of linen warp and woolen weft. The term has been mistakenly applied to worsted woolen quilted bed covers correctly described as calamanco or glazed camlet. See Calamanco.

Madder – a red dye from the plant *Rubia tinctorum*, a plant native to Asia Minor. Bluets and bedstraw, native American plants, are also members of the madder family but do not yield enough dye to make cultivation or collection of the plants worthwhile.

Mordant – an additive used to make a dye such as madder or cochineal colorfast. Alum, copperas and potassium dichromate are mordants.

Outline stitch – A running stitch, used by itself in embroidery and often used in conjunction with the darning stitches to outline the pattern before the motif was filled in with darning stitches.

Pattern darning – embroidery made by pattern darning in which the foundation fabric warps and wefts are worked under and over in regular sequence. The stitches are worked in repeated order forming geometrical designs on the top surface of the foundation fabric. This stitch does not make a raised pile.

Pile – formed by embroidery stitches to raise the yarn from the foundation fabric.

Plied – two or more strands twisted together.

Ply – one of the twisted strands of yarn.

Rose Blanket – a plain, common blanket, most often of natural color with embroidered circular design worked in each corner, so named as the design resembled the decorative compass rose motif on maps. Many were made between 1800 and 1850, some were imported and some were made in America. They were often listed in probate inventories.

Rug – a coarse wool fabric with a shaggy surface.

Running stitch – yarn carried in and out of the foundation fabric forming a line of stitches on both front and back surfaces.

Scotch carpet – ingrain carpeting that was made in Scotland. The *Boston Gazette* on Sept. 1, 1760 contained an add for "SCOTCH FLOOR CARPETS, Counterpins, Bed Ruggs…" (Dow p. 167).

Stem stitch – a back stitch worked with the yarn held below the needle forming a line of downward slanting stitches.

Stroke stitches – short, parallel stitches, straight or slightly oblique, forming parallel diagonal stitches on the surface of the foundation fabric. This stitch was used to make hearth rugs.

Tabby weave – plain weave or even weave, where the fabric's warp and weft pass over and under each thread.

Turkey work – needlework made in imitation of Turkish carpets. A pile fabric worked on a loom, with closely set knots of worsted yarn set into a heavy linen warp, held in place by weft rows of linen. In embroidery the stitch is made when the yarn is drawn through the foundation fabric in closely set stitches and knotted on the surface. In the *Boston Gazette* on May 26, 1755 an advertisement by Jarvis and Parker Store on King Street, Boston included "Turkey quilts" (Dow p. 164).

Turkish knot – Giordes knot used to make Oriental carpets. This can be made by several methods of knotting or wrapping the yarn around warps to form a pile in the weaving.

Twill or Tweel – a weave producing a diagonal effect in the finished fabric. Among the types of twill weaves are bird's eye, herringbone and diamond. Twilled wool was known as serge, twilled cotton as fustian or jean and twilled silk was known as satin.

Uncut Pile – looped, running stitch embroidery that leaves the pile uncut.

Warp – the yarns set into a loom that are wound on the back beam, tied to the front beam and crossed by the weft.

Weft – the filling yarns held in the shuttle and carried back and forth through the warp from selvedge to selvedge.

Woolen – fabric made with short staple, carded woolen yarn.

Worsted – fabric made with smooth, shiny, long staple, combed wool yarn, also used as a synonym for crewel or crewel yarn.

Yarn sewn – a technique used when referring to an embroidered textile, especially hearth or other small floor rugs or carpets.

Appendix

The Will of Mary (Chilton) Winslow

In the name of God Amen the thirty first day of July in the yeare of our Lord one thousand Six hundred seventy and Six I Mary Winslow of Boston in New England Widdow being weake of Body but of Sound and perfect memory praysed be almighty God for the same Knowing the uncertainty of this present life and being desirous to settle that outward Estate the Lord hath Lent me. I doe make this my last Will and Testamt in manner and forme following (that is to say) First and Principally I commend my Soule into the hands of Almighty God my Creator hopeing to receive full pardon and remission of all my sins, and Salvation through the alone merits of Jesus Christ my redeemer: And my body to th eEArth to be buried in Such Decent manner as to my Executor hereafter named shall be thought meet and convenient and as touching such worldly Estate as the Lord hath Lent me my Will and meaneing is the same shall be imployed and bestowed as hereafter in and by this Will is Exprest

Imps I doe hereby revoake renounce and make voide all Wills by me formerly made and declaire and apoint this my Last Will and Testamt Item I will that all the Debts that I Justly owe to any manner of person or persons whatsoever shall be well and truly paid or ordained to be paid in convenient time after my decease by my Executor hereafter named—Item I give and bequeath unto my Sone John Winslow my great Square table Item I give and bequeath unto my Daughter Sarah Middlecott my Best gowne and Pettecoat and my Silver beare bowle and to each of her children a Silver Cup with an handle: Also I give unto my grandchild William Paine my Great silver tankard: Item I give unto my Daughter Susanna Latham my long Table: Six Joyned Stooles and my great Cupboard: a bedstead Bedd and furniture there unto belonging that is in the Chamber over the roome where I now Lye, my small silver Tankard: Six Silver Spoones, a case of Bottles with all my wearing apparel: (except onely what I have hereby bequeathed unto my Daughter Meddlecott & my Grandchild Susanna Latham:) Item I give and bequeath unto my Grandchild Ann Gray that trunke of Linning that I have alreddy delivered to her and is in her possession and also one Bedstead, Bedd Boulster and Pillows that re in the Chamber over the Hall: Also the sume of ten pounds in mony to be paid unto her within Six months next after my decease: Also my will is that my Executor shall pay foure pounds in mony pr ann for three yeares unto Mrs. Tappin out of the Intrest of my mony now in Goodman Cleares hands for and towards the maintenance of the said Ann Gray according to my agreemt with Mrs. Tappin: Item I give and bequeath unto Mary Winslow Daughter of my sone Edward Winslow my largest Silver Cupp with two handles: and unto Sarah Daughter of the said Edward my lesser Silver Cupp with two handles: Also I give unto my Said Sone Edwards Children Six Silver Spoones to be divided between them: Item I give and bequeath unto my grandchild Parnell Winslow the Sume of five pounds in mony to be improved by my Executor until he come of age: and then paid to him with the improvemt. Item my will is that the rest of my spoones be divided among my grandcidren according to the discression of My Daughter Middlecott: Item I give unto my Grandchild Mercy Harris my White Rugg: Item I give unto my Grandchild Mary Pollard forty shillings in mony. Item I give unto my grandchild Susanna Latham my Petty Coate with the silke Lace: I give unto Mary Winslow Daughter of my Sone Joseph Winslow the Sume of twenty pounds in mony to be paid out of the sume of my said Sone Joseph now owes to be improved by my Executor for the said Mary and paid unto her when She Shall attaine the Age of eighteene yeares or day of Marriage which of them shall first happen Item I give and bequeath the full remainder of my Estate whatsoever it is or wheresoever it may be found unto my children Namely John Winslow Edward Winslow Joseph Winslow Samuel Winslow: Susanna Latham and Sarah Middlecott to be equally divided betweene them Item I doe hereby nominate constitute authorize and appoint my trusty friend Mr. William Tailer of Boston aforesd merchant the Sole

Executor of this my last Will and testamt: In Witness wherof I the said Mary Winslow have hereunto set my hand and Seale the daye and yeare first above written

Memorandum I do hereby also Give and bequeath unto Mr. Thomas Thacher paster of the third Church in Boston the Sume of five pounds in mony to be pd convenient time after my decease by my Executr.

Mary Winslow

M

Her marke

Singed Sealed and Published by the above named Mary Winslow as her Last Will & Testamt in the Presence of us after the adding of four lines as part of her will

John Hands

Ffrancis Hacker

Her H marke

John Hayward scr

Mr. Wm Tailer nominated. Execr appeared in Court pr May: 1679 and renounced his Executorship to this will

Attests. Jsa Addington Cler.

Extracted from the Mayflower Web Pages with the permission of Caleb Johnson. Transcriptions of wills and inventories of all Mayflower passengers may be found in Volume 1: *Wills and Probates Plymouth Colony Records: Volume1, 1633-1669,* edited by C.H. Simmons and published by Picton Press of Rockport, Maine.

The Will of Elizabeth (Tilley) Howland - 1686
of Plymouth Colony

In ye Name of God Amen I Elizabeth Howland of Swanzey in ye County of Bristoll in ye Collony of Plymouth in New Engld being Seventy nine years of Age but of good & perfect memory thanks be to Allmighty God & calling to Remembrance ye uncertain Estate of this transitory Life & that all fflesh must Yeild unto Death when it shall please God to call Doe make constitute & ordaine & Declare This my last Will & Testament, in manner & forme following Revoking and Anulling by these prsents all & every Testamt & Testamts Will & Wills heretofore by me made & declared either by Word or Writing And this to be taken only for my last Will & Testament & none other. And first being penitent & sorry from ye bottom of my heart for all my sins past most humbly desiring forgivenesse for ye same I give & Committ my soule unto Allmighty God my Savior & redeemer in whome & by ye meritts of Jesus Christ I trust & believe assuredly to be saved & to have full remission & forgivenesse of all my sins & that my Soule wt my Body at the generall Day of Resurrection shall rise againe wt Joy & through ye meritts of Christs Death & passion possesse & inheritt ye Kingdome of heaven prepared for his Elect & Chosen & my Body to be buryed in such place where it shall please my Executrs hereafter named to appoint And now for ye settling my temporall Estate & such goodes Chattels & Debts as it hath pleased God far above my Deserts to bestow upon me I Do Dispose order & give ye same in manner & forme following (That is to say) First that after my funerall Expenses & Debts paid wc I owe either of right or in Conscience to any manner of person or persons whatsoever in Convenient tyme after my Decease by my Execrs hereafter Names I Give & bequeath unto my Eldest Son John Howland ye sum of five pounds to be paid out of my Estate & my Booke called Mr Tindale's Workes & also one pair of sheetes & one pr of pilowbeeres & one pr of Bedblanketts. Item I give unto my son Joseph Howland my Stillyards & also one pr of sheetes & one pr pillobeeres Item I give unto my son Jabez Howland my ffetherbed & boulster yt is in his Custody & also one Rugg & two Blanketts yt belongeth to ye said Bed & also my great Iron pott & potthookes Item I give unto my son Isaack Howland my Booke called Willson on ye Romanes & one pr of sheetes & one paire of pillowbeeres & also my great Brasse Kettle already in his possession Item I give unto my Son in Law Mr. James Browne my great Bible Item I give & bequeath unto my daughter Lidia Browne my best ffeatherbed & Boulster two pillowes & three Blanketts & a green Rugg & my small Cupboard one pr of Andylrons & my lesser brasse Kettle & my small Bible & my booke of mr Robbinsons Workes called Observations Divine & Morrall & allso my finest pr of Sheetes & my holland pillowbeeres, Item I give unto my Daughter Elisabeth Dickenson one pr of Sheetes & one pr of pillowbeeres & one Chest Item I give unto my Daughter Hannah Bosworth one pr of sheetes & one pr of pillowbeeres, Item I give unto my Grand Daughter Elizabeth Bursley one paire of sheetes and one paire of Pillowbeeres Item I give & bequeath unto my Grandson Nathaniel Howland (the son of Joseph Howland) and to the heires of his owne Body lawfully begotten for ever all that my Lott of Land with ye Meadow thereunto adjoining & belonging lying in the Township of Duxbury neare Jones River bridge, Item I give unto my Grandson James Browne One Iron barr and on Iron Trammell now in his possession, Item I give unto my Grandson Jabez Browne one Chest Item I give unto my Grand Daughter Dorothy Browne my best Chest & my Warming pan Item I give unto my Grand Daughter Desire Cushman four Sheep, Item I give & bequeath my wearing clothes linen and Woollen and all the rest of my Estate in mony Debts linen or of what kind or nature or sort soever it may be unto my three Daughters Elizabeth Dickenson, Lidia Browne and Hannah Bosworth to be equally Devided amongst them, Item I make constitute and ordaine my loving Son in Law James Browne and my loving son Jabez Howland Executors of this my last Will and Testament, Item it is my Will & Charge to all my Children that they walke in ye Feare of ye Lord, and in Love and peace towards each other and endeavour the true performance of this my last Will & Testament In Witnesse wherof I the said Elizabeth Howland have hereunto sett my hand & seale this seventeeth Day of December Anno Dm one thousand six hundred Eighty & six.

The mark of Elisabeth   E H   Howland

Signed Sealed & Delivd

In ye prsence of us Witnesses

Hugh Cole

Samuel Vyall

John Browne

==

Extracted from the Mayflower Web Pages with the permission of Caleb Johnson. Transcriptions of wills and inventories from Plymouth Colony also can be found in *Plymouth Colony Records: Volume 1: Wills and Probates, 1633-1669* edited by C.H. Simmons, published by Picton Press of Rockport, Maine.

The Will of Mary VanSweringen
of Maryland

IN THE NAME OF GOD AMEN, I Mary Vansweringen of St. Maryes County Widdow
being Sick of body but of sound and perfect mind and memory thanks be to
Allmighty for the Same and Considering the uncertainty of this transitory
life we are in and that all mortals must dye do think convenient to settle
all such temporall Benefitts as it hath pleased Allmighty God to bless me
with in order thereunto doe make my last will and Testament Revokeing
Renouncing and making void all former will or Wills by me made and this
only to be my last will and testament first and principally I give and
bequeath my Soul to Allmighty God that gave it Constantly believing that
through the Meritorious Death and passion of my Blessed Savior Jesus
Christ I shall receive full pardon and remission of my Sins and
tansgretions past and my Body I bequeath to the Earth from when it Came
to be buried in Decent and Christian Maner as my Executor hereafter named
shall think fitt.
Item I Give and Bequeath unto my Loveing Daughter Dorithy VanSweringen
four negroes two feather beds two Ruggs two pair of blankets, two pair of
Sheets and two bolsters one Silver pint Cupp, Six Silver Spoons one Small
English Table to be Delivered to her at the Day of her marriage by my
Executor herafter Named;...
Item I Give and bequeath unto my Loving Daughter Tereshea VanSweringen
four Negroes, two feather beds two Ruggs two pair of Blanketts, two pair
of Sheets two bolsters one Pint Silver tankered Six Silver Spoons a Chest
of Drawers and a Small Looking Glass: and to Each of them my Said Daughters
a Suite of table linen all which to be Delivered to my said Daughters by my
Executor at the Day of their Marriage the above said Legacies being in full
satisfaction for their part or portion of their fathers and my Estate.
Item I Give and bequeath unto my loveing Son Joseph VanSweringen all that
 tract or parcel of Land lying in St. Maryes County near St Maryes Called
the point containing two hundred acres or thereabouts to him and his heirs
and assigns for Ever; my Said Son being and is to maintain my Said two
Daughters handsomly untill they are married.
Item I Give unto my loveing Son in Law Mr. William Bladen and my Daughter
Bladen a Ring of thirty shillings price to Each of them;
Item I Give and Bequeath unto My Loveing Daughter Elinor Carroll two
Thousand pound of Tobacco to be paid by my Executor in Convenient time
after my decease, it is my Desire that the Negroes which I have Given to My
two Daughters Shall be Such as my Said Executor think fitt they not
Exceeding forty years a piece;
Item I Give and Bequeath all the Rest of My Estate both Real and person
Unto my Said Son Joseph VanSweringen after all my Just Debts are paid and

Lastrly I doe hereby Constitute and appoint my loving Son Joseph
VanSweringen my whole and sole Executor of this my last will and testament
In witness wherof I have hereunto Sett my hand and Seale this Seaventeenth
Day of Febry 1712/13

Singed Sealed and Delivered in the
Presence of Wm Aisquith, Ann Moloni, Hannah (Her Mark) Bantom

MARY VANSWERINGEN (SEALE)
At ye foot of the afortegoing will was thus written, Sept 5 1713
Then Came Ann Moloni and Hannah Bantom two of the Witnesses to the within
will and made oath that they saw the within Named Mary VanSwearingen Signe
Seale and Deliver the Same as her last will and Testament...

                                    WM AISQUITH   Dept

Comissry

===

File contributed for use in USGenWeb Archives by Elizabeth F. Randolph. Mary
VanSweringen, nee Smith, was the second wife of Garrett VanSweringen. The will is on
file at Maryland State Archives, Hall of Records, Annapolis, Md. Prerogative Court
(wills) 13, pages 557 and 558, (MSA S538, MdHR 1291-4. 1-11-1-14).

The Will of John Barnet 1734
Lancaster County, Pennsylvania

JOHN BARNET
deceased

IN the name of God AMANE I John Barnet being weake but of perfect memory blefed
be God

I first commit my soul to the lord and my Boddey to the Grave my hope of a
betfed resurechon

first I leave to my well be loved Wife the sum of Twenty pounds to be payd out
of the Cattell & crop that is now on ye ground and the remainder of ye Crop
to maintain her & the family

and next I leave to my beloved Sons John and Joseph my plantation Equally
to be divided between them and if it please God that one of them Dy's the other
shall have it all ans in case that both dye I leave it to my Beloved sons
Robert & James equally to be divided but if it Please God to Spair John and
Joseph to the Years of Mattorety and John desire to have all the place it
shall be vallved by two Indifferent men and John shall pay to Joseph the half
of the said Vallve and I leave to my son John one Black year old C oult and to
John and Joseph I leave my Working horses namly one Hors & too mean to each
an equall part and to my Beloved daighther Rebeckah I leave one Bay hors Coult
cuning three year old and two cows to be given her afs the Stock when it will
Suit best with her Convnencey and my wifes – and to my befoued Daughter
Marey I leave one Black Mear six year old and if she live on the Place with her
mother and ye boys till she come to Age she shall then have two cows and in
case goes to her own hand she shall have but one cow when shee is of Age and
for and in consideration of Ten Pounds payd to me in hand by by son Robert I
leave my son Robert One hundred and fifty nine acres of land that is to say the
warrent right and survey which he hath now Jin pofeson on the South East End
of the land I leave and beqath to my Daughter Jean on Red Coulerd and white
faced Heffer Coming two year old and one rugo Or bed quilt this is my Will
and Testment given under my hand this first Day of July in ye Year of our
Lord and Savior Jefufus Christ 1734

Wittnes Present   Allexr. Davison,   James Whithill

I order ye Management of my affairs at my deceas into the hands of my well
beιoved Wife and my son Robit as Adminesterators and Guardens to the Children
whill under age.

Will proved Oct. 1, 1734

Extracted from the Will Book A, Vol. 1, page 15, Lancaster County, Pennsylvania Archives. Submitted
courtesy of the Southern Lancaster County Historical Society, Quarryville, Pa., and copied as it appeared in
the Lancaster archives by Marie Malark for the USGenWeb.

The Will of Peter Guerrant, The Huguenot
of Virginia

In the name of God, Amen. I Peter Guerrant of the parish of King William, in the county of Cumberland, being in health of body and of sound and disposing mind and memory, praise be Almighty God for the same, but considering the uncertainty of human life, do make this my last will and testament in manner following: That is to say, my just debts being paid first and satisfied.

Item: I give and bequeath to my eldest son John Guerrant Four hundred acres of land, lying on Jushua's [sic.] Creek, one of the branches of Slate river [sic.] in Albemarle County, for him and his heirs forever. I also give him, my son John Guerrant, a horse called Jockey and my Philadelphia saddle, for him and his heirs forever.

Item: I give and bequeath unto my son Peter Guerrant, four hundred acres of land lying and being on Hunt's Creek, one of the branches of the Slate river [sic.] in Albemarle County, for him and his heirs forever. I also give my son Peter Guerrant one feather bed and furniture for him and his heirs forever.

Item: I give and bequeath to my son Daniel Guerrant Four hundred acres of land joining on his brother John Guerrant's line, it being part of an order of Council for six hundred acres of land on Jushua's Creek, one of the branches of Slate river [sic.] in Albemarle County, for him and his heirs forever. I also give my son Daniel Guerrant one Negro boy named Caesar, for him and his heirs forever.

Item: I give unto my daughter Esther Guerrant Two hundred acres of land on Collier's line—it being part of the four hundred acres of land on Mountain Creek in Amelia County, for her and her heirs forever. I also give my daughter Esther Guerrant the other new bed, with what furniture there is to it, and a rug, and two cows and calves for her and her heirs forever, and two pounds of current money, and the two cows and calves to be delivered when she shall attain the age of twenty-one years or married.

Item: I give and bequeath to my daughter Magdalene Guerrant the other two hundred acres of land on Mountain Creek in Amelia County, it being the other part of the four hundred acres, for her and her heirs forever. I also give my daughter Magdalene Guerrant the sum of five pounds Current money to be paid out of my personal estate and two cows and calves, to be delivered after she shall attain the age of twenty-one years or married.

Item: I give and bequeath unto my daughter Jane Guerrant Two hundred acres of land, it being part of an order of Council for six hundred acres of land lying and being on Joshua's Creek, one of the branches of Slate River, in Albemarle County, for her and her heirs forever. I also give my daughter Jane Guerrant, the sum of Five pounds Current money, to be paid out of my personal estate, and two cows and calves, to be delivered after she shall attain the age of twenty-one years or married.

Item: I give and bequeath unto my daughter Judith Guerrant, the sum of fifteen pounds Current money for her heirs forever.

Item: If in case my wife Magdalene Guerrant should happen to be now with child, and it should happen to be a boy, I give him thirty-five pounds Current money, to be laid out of my personal estate, for him and his heirs forever, but, if it should happen that my beloved wife is with child of a daughter, my will is that I give her fifteen pounds Current money, for her and her heirs forever.

Item: I leave to my beloved wife Magdalene Guerrant, the use of the plantation I now live on, with the use of three negroes, Tom, Sarah, and Moll, during her natural life, and my will is that my beloved wife shall have the use of all the Negroes, during the time of her widowhood. Caesar only excepted which is before given to my son Daniel Guerrant, but in case that it should happen that there be not movable estate enough to satisfy the legacies before given, my will is that Betty shall be sold by way of outcry to satisfy the afore given legacies.

Item: My will is that after my beloved wife Magdalene's decease, that all the negroes and all the plantation I now live on shall be sold by way of outcry and the money be equally divided among my beloved children who will be living at that time.

Item: I do constitute and ordain my well beloved wife Magdalene Guerrant to be the whole and sole executrix of this my last will and testament, and I do hereby declare this and none other to be my last will and testament, revoking all other wills and testaments, which may have by me been formerly made. In witness wherof, I have hereto set my hand and fixed my seal, this Third day of December, One Thousand Seven hundred and forty-nine.

The will of Peter Guerant of Virginia was compiled by Ann Woodlief, and appears among other genealogical materials on the Geocities Heartland Internet site via Cyndi's List.

The Will of Francis Stringer,
Craven County, North Carolina 1749

In the name of God Amen I Francis Stringer of the Province and County
first mentioned____ being of soundmind and memory do this Eighth (sic.) day
of January in the year of our Lord One Thousand Seven Hundred and Forty-
nine make and publish this my last Will and Testament in Manner following
Viz? I will and devise that my wife Hannah STRINGER and my daughter
Elizabeth STRINGER should out of what I here after in- this will and
Testimony give and bequeath (?) them Equally pay my just debts and
funneral charges ___(that?) is___(that?) my said wife Hanah (sic.)
STRINGER should out of what by this will is left her pay the full one
half of my funneral Charges and debts, and that my said daughter Eliz'a
STRINGER out of what is left her by this will pay the other half of my
debts and funeral charges which I desire(?) my herein (?) after
mentioned Executors my Will be executed. I give and bequeath unto my dear
mother Mary STRINGER if living and Claiming by her self or any other
person for her within the ___space of ten years ___ the date ___ one
of my best featherbeds, one good rugg (sic.) one good pair of blankets,
one good pair of ___ (midling?) sheets, one good feather ____/ 2 pillows
one good pillow and one bed ___. (slide?) Two (midling?) sized Iron potts,
Twelve ___ puter plates, two ___ puter dishes, one good ___ of knives
and forks to be bought by my executors out of my personal estate and
delivered by them to her.   Likewise I give and bequeath unto my mother
Mary STRINGER if living and should come into this said Province or claim
to as above an my ---(stock?) of hogs are upon a plantation or belonging
there to which I formerly bought of Henry SUMMERLIN two cows and calves.
I further Will and desire that my said mother who in this Province shall
live upon said plantation. ___ which I bought of said Henry SUMMERLIN and
have to whose profits of said plantation and the use and labor of two
negroes to wit. of one negroe man called big Calvon? and of one negro
woman said C____ wife, Called Rose, during my said mothers natural life
and after her my said mother deceased, I devise and bequeath said
plantation and land containing three hundred acres unto my half brother
Ralph STRINGER his heirs and assigns forever provided he or his
representatives claims the said land within ten years after my said
mothers decease and the above said two negros afore (?) my said mothers
decase I give to my daughter Eliz STRINGER and in case my said mother
should not come into this Province and claims by herself or others any
part or parcel of any bequest or legacy left her before in this my Will it
is then my will and desior (design?) that my Executors here in after
mentioned should make sale of my land in Adams Creek and out of the money
arising from such sale pay unto my said mother if living and claiming by

92

herself or others one hundred pistales. I give and bequeath to Anne (GRIFFIN or COFFIN?) Widow four pounds shillings, I give and bequeath unto my brother in law John SHINE the one half of a tract of land I bought of Durham (?) Handcock lying on the East side of (Storey/Stoney Town Creek?) in Craven County and to his heirs and assigns forever. I further order and beseech? afor said land shall be divided, he should have his choice of which part he will except (sic.) of. I give and bequest unto my said brother in law John SHINE all sums of money is indebted to me at the date here of, my silver mounted _uttoe and all my book except the family books. I give desire and bequeath unto my brother William STRINGER to him his heirs and assigns forever all my lots in New Bern I own providing he or any person for him claims in ten years until such claims is made I give the rents and profits of said lots in New Bern to my daughter Elizabeth Stringer. I give and bequeath brother in law Daniel SHINE my land upon Upper Falling Creek in Johnston County in this Province to him his heirs and assigns forever. I give and bequeath unto John STRINGER a crippled boy son of George STRINGER of Coor (?) Creek in this county one Hundred and forty three pounds eleven shillings old bill money which his father George STRINGER is indebted to me which said sum of one hundred forty three pounds eleven shillings I devise my executors to buy cows and calves and take up a piece of land for said son in good place for cattle and put the cattle ___ on said land for the use of said John Stringer (See note below.) I give to my Executors hereafter mentioned one mourning Ring to each Executor each ring to be in __one ___ ___. I give to William Bond whatever sums of money that at this date he is indebted to me I give and bequeath unto my nephew Thos STRINGER son of my said brother Ralph STRINGER and unto my Allegitimate (sic.) Thos STRINGER equally to them their heirs forever providing they or any person for them claims in ten (?) years my land commonly called Dover containing more or less two hundred fifty acres and if any one of them or any person impowered by them shold claim before the other them it is my desire that my executors should lay off to him so claiming the full one half of my said land called Dover   I give bequeath unto my loving wife Hannah STRINGER Eight negroes to with one negro man called Joe Prince, one Negro man called Adam, one Negro called ___:, one negro man called old Jimmy, one molatto boy named Zekiel, one Molatto woman called Pat or Pegg, one Negro woman called Phillis, and one negro girl. Exetrs. DanOl shine James Green Thos ____

(On 15 Nov 1744 John STRINGER was deeded 100 acres Craven joining Abre Odam's land. DOBBS COUNTY NORTH CAROLINA ENTRIES AND WARRENTS 1741-1757 compiled by Wm. L. Murphy.)

The Will of Kirk Gunby
of Somerset County, Maryland 1775

In the name of God Amen, January the nineteenth day of Anno Donno One
Thousand Seventeen hundred and Seventy Five, I Kirk Gunby of Somerset
County in the Province of Maryland Plantation being in perfect mind and
memory thanks be to Almighty God for it and calling to mind the
uncertainty of this present life and willing to Settle my affairs here
on Earth and as for my Worldly Estate which it hath pleased God to bless
me with I bestow in name and form as followeth viz.

Imprimus I give and bequeath unto my son John Gunby to him and his heirs
and assign forever all that Tract of land called Middle Ridge and also
all that tract of marsh called Kirks Chance and also all my right of a
parcel of land or marsh which I bought of Ambrose Dixon on Jeans Island
Marshes known by the name of Dixons Lott and likewise all my right and
title of that parcel of land I bought of James Gunby out of a track of
land called Kirks Purchase and likewise all my right and title of two
tracts and land and marsh which I bout of Capt. John Williams at Jones
creek one tract known by the name of Flatt Caps the other by the name of
Mistake and likewise one half of the mill and also my Negro man named
Walt and also Negro girl named Grace and all my surviving clothes and
also my young mare called Jenny and fifteen pounds common money and my
Silver shoe buckles.

Item, I give and bequeath unto my son Levin Gunby to him and his heirs
and assign forever my Negro man Giddeon and also my Negro boy
named Andrew and also my Negro girl named Minta and also fifty acres of
marsh that I bought of Ambrose Dixon on Jeans Island Marsh.

Item, I leave unto my daughter in law Elizabeth Gunby widow of David
Gunby all my right and title of a tract of land called Crooked Lane in
now Sussex County during her natural life and also I leave to her my
Negro girl called Jemmy during her, the said widows natural life.

Item, I give and bequeath unto my grandson Stephen Gunby, son of David
Gunby after his mother's death all my right and title of a tract of land
called Crooked Lane wheron they now dwell to him and his heirs and
assign forever.
Item, I give and bequeath unto my grandson Kirk Gunby, son of David
Gunby after his mothers death my Negro girl named Jemmy and all her
increase after my death to him and his heirs and assign forever.

heirs and assign forever my Negro boy named George and also my young Negro woman named Juda and all her increase before the date of this will and after this date and also my Negro girl named Mina.

Item I give and bequeath unto my daughter Mary Cottingham to her and her heirs and assign forever my Negro man named Robin and also my Negro girl named Violet. Now after my lawful debts and legases being paid, for my daughter Mary Cottingham to allow out of her moveable part of my estate the sum of fifty eight pounds common money before she shares her part with the rest of my children it being for favors due her in times past.

Item I give and bequeath unto my son James Gunby one shilling Sterling money of Great Britain to him and his heirs forever.

Item I give and bequeath unto my daughter Sarah Goodman one shilling Sterling money of Great Britain to her and her heirs forever.

Item I give and bequeath unto my granddaughter Sarah Kirk Gunby to her and her heirs and assign forever my Negro girl named Milley and one feather bed, two sheets, two blankets and one rug and two pillows and two pewter dishes and six pewter plates and pewter basin and one cow and calf.

Item I give and bequeath unto my daughter in law Elizabeth Gunby, widow of Kirk Gunby to her and her heirs and assign forever fifteen pounds common money.

Item I leave unto my well beloved wife Sarah Gunby my Negro man named Tobe and my old woman Juda and my Negro girl named Hannah. It is my will and desire that after the decease of my beloved wife Sarah Gunby that old Negro Tobe and old Negro Juda may fall to be the property of my son John Gunby to him and his heirs and assign forever.

Item I leave unto my well beloved wife Sarah Gunby my Negro boy named Jacob during her natural life and after her decease I give and bequeath the said Negro Jacob unto my two daughters Sabra Potter and Mary Cottingham the them and their heirs and assign forever.

Item I give unto my well beloved wife Sarah Gunby one third part of my moveable estate items after my lawful debts and legases being paid and my wifes thirds made up I give and bequeath all the remainder of my estate to be equally dived between and amongst my three children that is to say Levin Gunby, Sabra Potter, and Mary Cottingham

children that is to say Levin Gunby, Sabra Potter, and Mary Cottingham
to them and their heirs and assign forever but for my daughter Sabra
Potter to allow out her part of my moveable estate the sum of twelve
pounds common money the* she shares her part with the rest of my children
it being for favors due her in times past.

Item I do hereby constitute appoint and ordain my son John Gunby to be
my whole and sole executor of this my last will and testament and I do
hereby revoke, disavow and dismissal of any other former wills or
testaments before made by me ratifying and confirming this and no other
to be my last will and testament in writing writing I have unto set my
hand and seal have affixed the day and year above written.

Kirk Gunby

Signed, sealed and acknowledged in the presence of us

Purnell Outten
Lazarus Lankford

===

* as written in the file

Somerset County Will EB1: 134
Kirk Gunby of Somerset County
Written 19 Jan 1775
Probated 12 June 1780
File contributed for use in USGenWeb Archives by Beth Johnson

The Will of Joseph Holmes   1762
Lunenburg County, Virginia

Page 332. Will. I, Joseph Holmes of L, very sick and weak –
First, all my lawful debts are to be paid.
To my brother, John Holmes' son, Thomas Holmes - all that
          tract of land on which I now live, allowing my wife one
          third part to live on, during her life. Also, I give to
          said Thomas Holmes a Negro boy named Camp, and one bay
          mare, one bay horse and saddle, and one bed, 2
          blankets, and one rug and 6 plates and 3 dishes, one iron
          pot and two thirds of my hogs and cattle, six chairs,
          and all the working tools on the plantation.
To my wife - one gray horse and one side saddle and bridle. And
          during her life, one third of my hogs and cattle.
To my daughter-in-law Ann Turner - 2 sheep.
To my son-in-law Edmon Turner - 2 sheep.
To my cousin Thomas Holmes - the rest of my estate.
I do not want my estate appraised.
Executor - my cousin Thomas Holmes.
Signed Dec. 17, 1761 - Joseph Holmes (+++ his mark).
Witnesses - William Baughan, Thomas Baughan, Joseph Hunt
William Glass (W his mark).
 At Feb. 2, 1762 Court, the will of the deceased was
exhibited by the executor, and proved by the oaths of three of
the witnesses, wherupon. on the motion of said executor,
probate of said will is granted him, and Rosemond (sic.) Holmes,
widow and relect of said testator, by deed signed with her
hand Feb. 1, 1762, and proved in Court by two witnesses,
does renounce and disclaim all benefit and advantage she
might have by means of any legacy bequeathed to her in said
will, which is ordered to be recorded.
 This deed witnesses that a considerable part of the estate
that Joseph Holmes possessed of, came by this marriage
with me and as he has not made, in his will, a sufficient

provision for my support, he having no children, I rely on the provision the law has made for the relief of the distressed, and I will not accept the legacies to me bequeathed, and do renounce all benefit of such will. Signed, Feb. 1, 1762 – Rosmond (sic.) Holmes (R her mark). Witnesses - Joseph Hunt, John Fuqua, Thomas Holmes.

Extracted from *Will Book No. 1 With Inventories, Accounts, Etc. 1746-1762*, Lunenburg County, Virginia, from a transcription made and produced for the Internet by TLC Genealogy, P.O. Box 403369, Miami Beach, Florida 33140-1369.

The Inventory of the Estate of Daniel Firth
Lunenburg County, Virginia 1751

Page 121. Inventory of the estate of Daniel Firth, deceased.
Includes 1 beaver trap, 1 bed and furniture, 1 feather bed
with bolster, 2 pillows, rug, blanket, 2 sheets, 6 books, a
pair of money scales. Total £ 23.3.5. We, David Gwin,
Jos. Perrin, and Saml Perrin, appraisers, appraised the
estate on Oct. 16, 1751. Signed – Jos. Perrin,
Saml Perrin,
Thos. Jones Adm'r.

===

Extracted from the *Will Book No. 12*, p. 121, *With Inventories, Accounts, Etc. 1746-1762*,
Lunenburg County, Virginia from a transcription made and produced for the Internet by
TLC Genealogy, P.O. Box 403369, Miami Beach, Florida 33140-1369.

Inventory of Goods and Effects of James Barber Deceased of Pennsylvania

Inventory of Goods and Effects of James Barber Deceased. Filed the 25th day of November 1768
#1253

Richard Rue and William Goslin Do you swear that You will well and Faithfully appraise and post a just and True Value upon the Goods, Chattles, Rights and Credits of James Barber Deceased, as they shall be shown or made known to you, without favour, affection --- or ill will so help you God

Taken before me this 7th day of November 1768
Thomas Barnsley

A Bill of an Appraisment Mde this 7th Day of November 1768 of the Estate
both Goods and Chattels of James Barber Lately Deceased of
Bristol Township Bucks County

To Wearing Apparrel Riding horse Bridle and Saddle		14-00-00
To A large pot two trambles a Kettle tongs and fire shovel		01-00-00
To a Little table and Dough Trough		00-09-00
To Six Chairs		00-10-00
To a pair of Lrge Hillards frying pan 3 plates		
– trenchers 2 bucketts		01-00-00
To a feather Bed Bedding and Bedstead		06-00-00
To a Little Spinning Wheel Box Chest and trunk		00-12-00
To a Rugg and Blankett		00-15-00
To a Chest Seeding Basket half Hogshead		
and old Barrel		00-09-00
To a CutLass		00-03-00
To two sives		00-02-06
To Nine Bushels of Rye thereabouts at 3/6 pr bushel		01-11-06
To About Nine Bushels of Indian Corn		01-04-09
To five Bushels of Hog Corn at –76 pr. Bushell		00-07-06
To One Bushel of Buck Wheat		00-02-06
To a Large Spinning Whhel and Cheese Press		00-01-00
To a plough Shear two Hoes --- Wedges and Sundrys		00-08-00
To a Plough Harrow and Working Gears		01-10-00
To a Drawing Knife a Saw two Rings and Sundrys	00-02-00	
To a --- Cow Bell and Collar		04-10-00
To a Brown Cow	03-10-00	
To a Red Heffer and a White faced Heffer		02-10-00
To a White Heffer		02-00-00

To five Yearlings		03-09-00
To a Red Fat Cow		04-10-00
To a Red calf		00-18-00
To a Bay Mare		00-15-00
To a Cross Saw and Loom Unseen by the Praisers	00-15-00	
To three White Shoats		00-15-00
To Wheat in the Barracks Supposed to be 18 Bushels		04-10-00
(total for page)		58-02-09
To a Barrack of Hay		06-00-00
To a Stack of Hay		02-10-00
To 4 Acres of Indian Corn 15 Bushels pr acre at		
2/ pr Bushel		06-00-00
To Six Acres of Green Wheat in Ground		06-00-00
To two Rakes and two forks		00-02-00
(Total for page)		20-12-00
Brought over		58-02-09
Total Sum		78-14-09

The inventory of James Barber, deceased, of Bristol Township, Bucks County, Pennsylvania.
Extracted from the USGenWeb Archives with permission of contributor, Donna Evans.

102

The Inventory of Noah Porter – 1790
Coventry, Connecticut

An inventory of the Estate of Mr. Noah
Porter late of Coventry deceas'd –

Wearing Apparel

	£	s	d
Bever hat 21s/ old do. 4s/ Perriwig 8s/ gold Shoe Buttons 18s/	£ 2	11	
3 Silver Buckles 6s/ five linnen shirt 10s/ two silk Hdfs. (?) 3s/	0	19	
3 Night Caps 6/ Surtout 15s/ Velour Waistcoat 5s/ Camblet do 1s/9	1	2	3
2 Linnen Hdfs.2s/ (?) breeches 4s/6 blue velour do. 7s/6	-	14	-
Broadcloth Cloak 36s/ black Coat & Waistcoat 40s/ old breeches 2s/	3	18	
Brown Coat 4s/6 Waistcoat 4s/ pr of Shoes 3s/ four pr stockings 7s/		18	6

Household Furniture--

	£	s	d
Case of Draws 90s/ do. with a Crown 75s/ Stand Table 24s/...............	9	9	
Round Table 20s/ two Candle Stands 17s/ five square tables 13s/	2	10	
Six Chests 21s/6 one great Chair & five fraimed Chairs 20s/	2	1	6
1 Windsor chair 8s/ five banester back chairs 12s/6 (?) flat do. 12s/	1	12	6
Feather Bed No. 1 Pillow & Bolster 80s/ Bedsted underbed and Cord 10s/ curtains 35s	6	5	
Feather Bed No. 2 Pillows and Bolster 80s/ Bedsted & Cord 8s/	4	8	
Feather Bed No. 3 Pillows & Bolster 54s/ Bedsted & Cord 5s/ Curtains 30s/	4	9	
Bed No. 4 old feathers Bedsted & Cord 36s/ Two Bed Quilts 40s/	3	16	
Rug 20s/ Coverled 7s/ one do. 3s/ two cheked Blankets 8s/	1	18	
Woolen Sheets 26s/6 two half Blankets 6s/ one Blanket 8s/	2	0	6
18 Linnen Sheets 49s/ three Holland do. 10s/6 25 pillow cases 29s/3	4	8	9
3 Table Cloaths 12s/ three do. 9s/ one large do. 10s/ Eight towels 8s/	1	19	
Looking Glass 48s/ one do. 2s/ four Window Curtains 9s/	2	19	
7 Large Silver Spoons 100s/ Six Tea do. 18s/ fifteen earthen plates 7s/	6	5	
8 Earthen Bowls 7s/ Tea Pot 1s/ Mug (?) 2s/ set of Tea Cups 1s/		11	
Cream Pot /6 Froot Glass /6 pewter Tankard 2s/ six pewter platters 19s/3	1	2	6
Seven pewter Plates 5s/6 Eight Pewter Basons 7s/6 two pewter Cups 3s/6	0	16	6
Tin Strainer 2s/ three tin Pans 2s/ water Pot 2s/ pint measure /9		6	9
2 Iron Kettles 8s/ Copper Kettle 6s/ brass Kettle 8s/ one do. 30s/	2	4	9
Skillet 2s/6 bake Pan 6s/ Spider 2s/6 flat Irons 6s/ three Tramels 12/	1	9	
Tongs 4s/ two fire Shovels 3s/ Handirons 13s/6 one do. 9s/6	1	10	
Hand Bellows 1s/6 Cheese Basket 1s/ Tobacco Box 2s/ Steely ards 3s/ ...		7	6
2 Hatchets 12s/ Bon Iron 1s/ brass Pan 3s/ five milk Pans 5s/	1	1	
2 Stone Jugs 4s/ four Stone Pots 4s/ three Pails 4s/ Sieve 1s/3		13	3
Bread Tub 1s/ two Trays 2s/6 Culer Tub 4s/ tin knives & forks 6s/		13	6
Shears /6 two cloaths Baskets 4s/ Butcher Knife 1s/ four Glass Bottles 2s/		7	6
Three Iron Basons 4s/ Frying Pan 2s/ Brush 1s/		7	
Part of a Barrel of Pork 33s/4 Meat Barrel 3/ 24/no/6 Ham (?) 69s/10	5	6	6

Gun 6s/ Sword 3s/ Loom, Warping Bars, Quil wheel Swifts
(?) 8 / 10 / .... 2 9 -
Foot Wheel 12s/ Eight Cyder Barrels 10s/6 two Reeds 10s/
Sheep Shears 1s/ 1 13 6
1 lb. Of Cotton wool 2s/ -42 lb. Bar Iron 11s/3 old Whip Saw 3s/4 .... 16 7
Iron Bar 8s/ Beetle Rings Iron Wedge and Pitchfork 6s/
Grindstone & Crank 6s/ .... 1 - -
Hive of Bees 2s/1 - 3 ½ lb. Sole Leather 2s/8 part of Calf Skin 5s/ 1 11 8
240 lb. of Lean Swine 46s/8 Saddle 8s/ Saddle Bags 5s/ 10 tons
of Hay 180s/ 11 19 8
Two old Bibles 5s/ Singing Book 2s/ 2 Vols Flavels Works 6s/ .... 13 -
Old Saw Mill Saw 6s/ Coverled 9s/ .... 15 -

                                                          £ 103 12 10

Two Oxen £10..10..- one Cow £3/18/- red white faced Cow £3..4.. ... 17 12
Black white faced Cow £3..12.. red cow £ 2..15. .... 6 7 -
Brindle cow £2..14.. pale red cow £3..6. .... 6 - -
Mare £9..0.. two year old Colt £6..6.. year old colt £ 5..0.. .... 20 6 -
Two Grist Mills Saw Mill with the Priviledge of the Stream .... 330 - -
106 ¾ acres of Land near the Meetinghouse with the Buildings 100/ ..... 533 15 -
12 ¾ acres of Land the opposite side of the High Way from the House 86/ 51 - -
41 ½ acres of Land laying near Bennet Fields 85s/ .... 176 7 -
18 acres of Land the south side of the Cross Street so calld. 80s/ .... 72 - -
108 acres acres of Land a little East E(?) Kingsbury Esqr. 78s/ .... 421 4 -
28 acres of Land West of Kingsbury @ 68s/ .... 95 4 -
51 acres Land laying in the Town of Mansfield @ 55s/ .... 140 5 -
26 ¾ acres of Land in the Town of Willington @ 40s/ .... 53 10 -
Allerton Cushman's Note 3 10 6
Town Order .... - 6 -
Note against the Inhabitants of the first Society in Coventry .... 12 3 -
582 Dollars Continental Money 15 9
The foregoing is a true Inventory of all the ˌstate of
                                                          £ 2044 7 7

Mr. Noah Porter late of Coventry deceasd shown to us by the Executor
And approved by us the Subscribers under Oath -------

                                        Benjamin Strong
Dated in Coventry Sept. 15th 1790   Eliass (?) Palmer   Appraisers

Entered & Recorded by Silvester Gilbert Clerk   John Hale

Transcribed from the Coventry, Connecticut Probate Records located at the Bolton Town
Hall, Bolton, Connecticut.

104

The Inventory of Simpson Jones Jr. 1835
Franklin County, Indiana

An inventory of the goods chattels and effects of Simpson Jones (Jr.) late of Franklin County and State of Indiana deceased taken by David Mount administrator of the estate the said deceased with the assistance of Isaac Wilson and John McWhorter appraisers called and duly sworn to that purpose.

1 lot of cupboard ware	3.00
1 lot of glass ware	1.00
1 lot of tin ware	1.50
1 iron ladle, 1 flesh fork & 1 lot of spoons	.75
1 lot of knives & forks	1.50
1 cupboard	3.50
1 lot of potters ware	1.00
1 lot of chairs (4 large, 1 small)	1.25
1 fire shovel, 1 pr andirons & 1 pot hangers	1.50
1 breakfast table	3.50
1 looking glass	.50
1 bureau	11.00
1 mantle clock	15.00
1 large bible & 1 ?	3.50
1 fancy bedstead	3.00
1 common do & cord	1.25
1 do do (upstairs)	1.00
1 do do do	1.00
1 bed & bedding upstairs	1.00
1 do do on fancy bedstead	13.00
1 do do and curtains	15.00
1 do do on low bedstead	17.50
10 yards blanketing	9.50
1 flowered bedspread	2.00*
1 birdseye coverlet	1.00
8 ½ yards janes	6.37 ½
2 calico quilts	3.00
1 single blue & white coverlet	2.50
2 white blankets	3.00
2 do do cotton Jacob	3.75
7 sheets	5.00
1 upper part for a quilt	.25
1 pine chest	.50
1 bbl with vinegar in it	2.00
9 ½ yds fulled cloth	9.50
2 sugar kettles	3.00
1 small brass kettle	.75

2 cake ovens & 1 cull	1.25
3 skillets	1.00
1 pot & 1 tea kettle	.75
1 gridiron	.75
2 washing tubs	.75
1 washing machine	.37 ½
1 large spinning wheel	2.00
1 churn	1.00
1 coffee mill	.75
½ part of cross cut saw & file	3.00
1 mans saddle	7.00
1 womans do	13.00
1 spinning wheel	2.00
1 reel	1.00
5 mill bags	2.25
4 bbl died (sic.) apples	8.75
1 do peaches	4.00
4 ½ bushels rye	1.12 ½
1 lot pickled pork	6.00
1 meat tub	.75
[page 54]	
2 empty tubs	.25
1 tub mackerel	1.00
1 pine bucket	.37 ½
1 rake & 3 spreading forks	.37 ½
1 hand saw	1.50
2 padlocks	.50
1 chopping axe	.75
1 sythe & cradle	2.00
1 cutting box	2.00
1 shovel plough & clevis & single tree	1.75
1 large plow	4.00
2 empty barrels	.12 ½
1 lot of gears	10.00
1 flax brake	.12 ½
1 double tree & single tree	.25 ½
1 lot gears & bridle	5.00
1 weeding hoe	.25
1 wagon	80.00
1 lot corn in the crib	90.00
2 stacks hay	12.00
2 do do near the meadow	15.00
1 lot flax	1.75
1 large white faced steer	15.00
1 white cow & her calf	112.00

1 brindle cow	9.00
1 white faced heifer	9.00
1 black & white do	9.00
1 red cow & her calf	13.00
1 brindle bull	3.00
1 black heifer	3.00
1 white bull	2.00
1 bay 2 yr old filley	27.00
1 brown 1 yr old do	18.00
1 claybank 2 yr old do	30.00
1 bay mare	60.00
1 bay gelding	60.00
1 stack oats	7.00
balance of 3 stacks wheat after taking out 16 bu	40.00
6 sheep 1st choice	7.00
15 do last do	15.00
27 fat hogs 1st choice	40.00
4 do do 2nd choice	7.50
53 stock hogs	15.00
7 hogs (5 in the open)	10.00
25 geese	6.25
1 goat	1.00
1 lot of apples	4.00
1 lot of salt	2.00
1 lot of wheat on the ground	12.00
1 lot of rye on the ground	25.00
1 slate	.25
1 shot pouch & powder horn	.25
	$1013.62 ½
1 ox yoke	2.00
1 iron wedge	.50
	$1016.12 ½

given under our hands this 20th day of December 1833
John McWhorter
Isaac Wilson   appraisers

To the above may be added	
James Roberts note	13.06 ¼
account against William Calfee	2.00
do do Isaac Frost	3.50
do do Lewis W. Clark	1.50
do do Simpson Jones Sr.	1.87 ½
Making in all	$1038.06 ¼

* This bed cover might have been an embroidered bed rug or worked (crewel) bed cover, as the description differentiates this cover from the quilts and coverlets listed in this inventory.

Extracted from the transcriptions of probate inventories made by Gary Stanton from the Court House in Brookville, Franklin County, Indiana for dissertation research between 1980 and 1984.

Advertisement for Winstead Academy
Winstead, Connecticut, 1812

Winstead Academy

The school of this place will be opened for
The ensuing season on the 9th of December
next, under the charge of MR. CURTIS WARNER
A.M. whose character and ability as an instruc-
tor need no comment. The languages preparatory to entrance into College, and such other
branches of literature as are usually attended to
in similar schools will be taught. Arrangements
are made for boarding on reasonable terms, and
in respectable families.
   JAMES BEACH,
   JAMES BOYD,   Trustees
   BISSELL HINSDALE,
   GRINNELL SPENCER,
Hartford, Nov. 28, 1812

Advertisement from the *Connecticut Courant*, Tuesday, December 8, 1812, Hartford, Connecticut: Volume XLVIII, No. 2498. Page 4 of 4 unnumbered pages. Printed by Hudson & Goodwin.

School for Young Ladies

Miss Hart's school for young ladies, re
commences on the 17th of May, in which,
as formerly, will be taught spelling, reading,
writing, (after Towne's method) English grammar, geography, arithmetic, composition, history, needlework on lace and muslin, embroidery,
and painting. A few young ladies, may be ac-
commodated with board in the family with the
preceptress, who assures those parents who may
place their daughters under her care, that her
unremitting endeavours shall not be wanting
(both in and out of school) towards improving
their minds and manners.
    Berlin, May 3, 1814.

Advertisement from the *Connecticut Courant*, Hartford, Tuesday May 24, 1814,
Volume L, No. 2575, page 4 of 4 unnumbered pages. Printed by Hudson & Goodwin.

Advertisement of Morris Academy for
Young Ladies in Connecticut

MORRIS-ACADEMY

A SCHOOL will commence at Morris-
Academy, in South Farms, for the re-
ception of young Ladies under the tuition of
Miss Olivia Bennett, on the 19th day of
May next; where the following useful
branches of education will be taught, viz
English Grammar, Geography, Arithmetic,
Rhetoric, Composition, Needlework, and
Painting. A strict attention will be paid
to morals. The Rev. William R. Weeks
School for Languages and the higher branches of English education, will be continued in said academy, as heretofore; His
summer term will commence the 9th day
of June.

South Farms, April 16

Advertisement from the *Connecticut Courant*, Hartford Connecticut, Tuesday, May 20,
1817, Vol. LIII, No 2730, page 1 of 4 unnumbered pages. Printed by George Goodwin &
Sons, Hartford.

Advertisement for Young Ladies Boarding School
Hartford, Connecticut

New Boarding-School

MRS. VALUE respectfully informs the public, that she proposes opening a BOARD-ING SCHOOL for young ladies on the first Monday in January next, when she will recommence teaching those branches of instruction, which she formerly taught young ladies with success, for a period of 15 years – viz. orthography, reading prose and verse, writing, arithmetic, *parsing* English grammar, the elements of astronomy on the celestial globe, geography on the terrestrial globe, with a correct knowledge of the atlas and maps, history, Blair's lectures, composition, drawing, painting, plain sewing, needle-work on muslin, and embroidery – in addition to which Mr. Value will give them a lesson every day (Sundays excepted) in polite manners, dancing, the French language, and music. Terms for board and tuition, $3 per week – it being understood, that each young lady will furnish herself with whatever will be necessary to use in school (the globes, atlas, and piano excepted): also her own wood and candles, when she is not with the family.

To say any thing on the utility of a good education would be superfluous; suffice, that this opportunity unites, upon reasonable terms, many of the useful and refined parts of a modern education for ladies.

According to the former custom in Mrs. Value's school, the young ladies will read once in the bible each day.

The number of boarders shall be limited to twenty, and attention, and who, it is presumes, will find the family and accommodations agreeable and satisfactory.

Hartford, November 29.

Advertisement in the *Connecticut Courant,* Hartford, Connecticut, Tuesday, Dec. 14, 1818, page 4 of 4 unnumbered pages, printed by Hudson & Goodwin Vol. XLIX, No. 2551.

Bibliography

A
Antiques. "Notes on Certain Early Covers". Editor. Vol. XII, November 1927.
Antiques. "All Wool and Wide". Editor. Vol. XXVI, November 1934.

B
Baker, Muriel L. *A Handbook of American Crewel Embroidery*. Rutland, Vt. and Tokyo, Japan: Charles E. Tuttle Co., 1966.

Benes, Peter, Editor. *Early American Probate Inventories*: Dublin Seminar for New England Folk Life, annual proceedings. Boston: Boston University Press, 1987.

Bernstein, David J. *The Mystery of the Bayeux Tapestry*. London: Guild Publishing Co., 1986.

Best, Muriel, Vicky Lugg and Dorothy Tucker. *Needlework School*. Secaucus, N.J. and London: Chartwell Books, 1984.

Bird, Caroline. *Enterprising Women, Their Contributions to the American Economy 1776-1976*. New York: W.W. Norton & Co., 1976.

Bowne, Eliza. *A Girl's Life Eighty Years Ago-Selections from the letters of Eliza Bowne*. New York: Scribner's Sons, 1888.

Burnham, Harold B. and Dorothy K. Burnham. *Keep Me Warm One Night Handweaving in Eastern Canada*. Toronto, Canada and Buffalo, N.Y.: University of Toronto Press, 1972.

C
Camin, Betty J. *Estate Records of Beaufort County, North Carolina*. Chelsea, Mich.: BookCrafters, 1984.

Caulfield, S. (Sophia) F. (Frances) A. (Anne) and Blanche C. Saward. *The Dictionary of Needlework: An Encyclopedia of Artistic, Plain and Fancy Needlework*. First printed in London in 1882 in two volumes. New York: Crown Publishers, 1972. A reprint of the 1887 edition.

Chase, A.W., M.D. *Dr. Chase's Recipes or Information for Everybody*. Ann Arbor, Mi.: 27th edition, 1866.

Clabburn, Pamela. *Samplers*. No. 30. Aylesbury, Bucks. England: Shire Publications Ltd., 1977.

Clabburn, Pamela. *Needleworker's Dictionary*. London: The MacMillan Co., 1976.

Connecticut Courant. Hartford, Ct., July 6, 1808.

Cummings, Abbott Lowell. "Notes on Furnishing the Seventeenth Century House." *Old Time New England* – The Bulletin of the Society for the Preservation of New England Antiquities, January-March 1956.

D
Davis, Mildred J. editor, and Valentine Museum Textile Resource and Research

Center, Richmond, Va. coauthors. *Embroidery Designs*. New York: 1971.

     Dow, George Francis. *Everyday Life in Massachusetts Bay Colony*. New York: Dover Publications, Reprint of 1935 edition, 1988.

     Dow, George Francis. *Domestic Life in New England in the Seventeenth Century*. New York: Benjamin Blom Inc., 1972. First published in 1925.

     Dow, George Francis. "The Patchwork Quilt and Some Other Quilts." *Old Time New England* – The Bulletin of the Society for the Preservation of New England Antiquities, April 1927.

     Dow, George Francis. *The Arts and Crafts of New England 1704-1775*. New York: Plenum Publishing Corp., 1967. Reprint of edition from Wayside Press, Topsfield, Ma.

E

Emery, Susan Anna. *Reminiscences of a Nonagenarian*. Newburyport, Ma.: William Huse & Co., 1879.

     Evans, Ruby. *Embroidery from Traditional English Patterns*. London and Newton Centre, Ma.: B.T. Batsford Ltd., London, Charles T. Branford Co., Newton Centre, Ma., 1971.

F

Farnam, Charles H. *History and Descendants of John Whitman of Weymouth, Ma.* New Haven, Ct.: Tuttle, Morehouse and Taylor, 1889.

     Felt, Joseph G. *The Customs of New England*. New York: Burt Franklin Co., 1970. A reprint of the 1853 edition.

     Foote, Abram. *Foote Family* Volume 1. Rutland, Vt.: Marble City Press – The Tuttle Co., 1907.

     Foote, Abigail. *The Diary of Abigail Foote June 2, 1775 to Sept. 15, 1775*, manuscript. Connecticut Historical Society.

     Foote, Elizabeth. *The Diary of Elizabeth Foote June 1, 1775 to Oct. 29, 1775.* manuscript. Connecticut Historical Society.

G

Giffen, Jane C. "Susanna Rowson and Her Academy." *Antiques,* September 1970.

     Goodwin, Nathaniel. *The Foote Family or The Descendants of Nathaniel Foote*. Hartford, Ct.: Press of Case & Tiffany Co., 1849.

     Gottesman, Ruth Susswein. *The Arts and Crafts of New York 1726-1776*. New York: The New York Historical Society, 1938.

     Gottesman, Ruth Susswein. *The Arts and Crafts of New York 1777-1779*. New York: New York Historical Society, 1954.

     Grant, Anne MacVicar. *Memoirs of an American Lady with Sketches of Manners and Scenery in America as they Existed Previous to the Revolution*. New York: The D. Appleton Co., 1846.

H

Hackenbrock, Y. *English and Other Needlework, Tapestries and Textiles in the Irwin Untermeyer Collection*. London: Thames and Hudson and the Metropolitan Museum of Art, 1962.

Harris, Estelle M.N. "A Pedigree Antique." *Antiques,* November 1927.

Hebron, Ct. Probate Records. Vol. 1, 1784-1796; Vol. 2, 1796-1803 including the records for the towns of Bolton, Columbia, Coventry, Hebron and Lebanon. Bolton Town Hall, Bolton, Ct.

Hedlund, Catherine A. *A Primer of New England Crewel Embroidery*. Sturbridge, Ma.: Old Sturbridge Village, 1963.

Hemenway, Abby Maria. *The Vermont Gazetteer*. Burlington, Vt.: published by A.M. Hemenway, 1867.

Holme, C. (Charles) Geoffrey. *A Book of Old Embroidery* with articles by A.F. Kendrick, Louisa F. Pesel & E.W. Newberry, Geoffrey Holme, editor. England: The Studio Ltd., 1921.

Howe, Margery Burnham. *Deerfield Embroidery*. New York: Charles Scribner's & Sons, 1976.

Hughes, Therle. *English Domestic Needlework*. London: Abbey Fine Arts, undated.

Huish, Marcus B. *Samplers and Tapestry Embroideries*. New York: Dover Publications Inc. reprint of second edition of 1913, 1970.

I

Iverson, Marion Day. "The Bed Rug in Colonial America." *Antiques,* January 1964.

J

Jerome, Brenda Joyce. *Caldwell County, Ky. Will Book B (1835-1889)* Evansville, Ind.: Evansville Bindery Inc., 1995.

Johnson, Samuel. *Dictionary of the English Language*. New York: A reprint by Barnes & Noble Co., 1994.

K

Kendrick, A.F. (Albert Frank). *English Needlework*. England: A.C. Black Ltd., 1933.

Kent, W.W. (William Winthrop*). A Primer of Hooked Rug Design*. Springfield, Ma.: Pond-Ekberg Co., 1941.

Kent, W.W. (William Winthrop). *The Hooked Rug*. New York: The Mead Co., 1930.

L

Lambert, Miss. *The Handbook of Needlework*. Philadelphia, Pa.: J.L. Gihon Co., 1854.

Landon, Mary Taylor and Susan Burrows Swan. *American Crewelwork*. New York: The Macmillan Co., 1970.

Lederer, Richard N. Jr. *Colonial American English*. Essex, Ct., A Verbatum Book, 1985.

M

Manwaring, Charles William. *A Digest of the Early Connecticut Probate Records*, Vol. 1, 1635-1700. Baltimore, Md.: Genealogical Publishing Co., 1904.

Marshall, Jessie A. "Bed Ruggs." *Yankee,* November 1977.

Montgomery, Florence M. *Textiles in America 1650-1870*. New York: The W.W. Norton & Co., a Winterthur/Barra book, 1984.

Morrison, Samuel Eliot. "Mistress Glover's Household Furnishings at Cambridge, Ma. 1638-1641." *Old Time New England* – Bulletin of the Society for the Preservation of New England Antiquities, July 1934.

N

Nevison, John L. *Catalogue of English Domestic Embroidery*. London: Victoria and Albert Museum, 1938.

R

Ring, Betty. "The Balch School in Providence, R.I." *Antiques*, April 1975.

S

Savage, James. *A Genealogical Dictionary of the First Settlers of New England Showing Three Generations of Those Who Came Before May 1692, on the Basis of Farmer's Register*. 4 volumes. Boston: 1860-62. Baltimore, Md. Genealogical Publishing Co. Inc., 1990.

Schuette, Marie and Sigrid Muller-Christensen (trans by Donald King). *A Pictorial History of Embroidery*. Westport, Ct.: Praeger Co., 1964.

Small, Walter Herbert. *Early New England Schools*. Boston and London: Ginn and Co. Publishers, 1914.

Stocking, Rev. Charles Henry Wright D.D. *The History and Genealogy of the Knowltons of England and America*. New York: The Knickerbocker Press, 1897.

Spooner, Thomas. *Records of William Spooner of Plymouth, Ma. and His Descendants*. Volume 1. Cincinnati, 1883.

Swan, Susan Burrows. *A Winterthur Guide to American Needlework*. New York: Crown Publishers, 1976.

Swan, Susan Burrows. *Plain and Fancy*. New York: Holt, Rinehart & Winston Co., 1977.

T

Taylor, Gertrude. "Mrs. Susanna Rowson, 1762-1824: An Early English-American Career Woman." *Old Time New England* – Bulletin of the Society for the Preservation of New England Antiquities, April 1945.

Townshend, Elizabeth M. *Early American Embroidery Designs*, an 1815 Manuscript Album with over 190 patterns. New York: Dover Publications, 1985.

U

Untermyer, Irwin and co-author Yvonne Hackenbroch. *English and Other Needlework, Tapestries and Textiles in the Irwin Untermyer Collection.* Boston: Published for the Metropolitan Museum of Art by Harvard University Press, 1960.

U.S. Department of Commerce and Labor, Bureau of Census, *Heads of Families at the First Census in the United States in 1790, Connecticut Cens*us. Washington, D.C.: Government Printing Office, 1908.

V

Vanderpool, Emily Noyes. *Chronicle of a Pioneer School from 1792 to 1833. Being a History of Miss Sarah Pierce and Her Litchfield School.* The 1903 edition edited by Elizabeth C. Barney Buel. Cambridge, Ma.: The University Press, 1943.

Vanderpool, Emily Noyes. *More Chronicles of a Pioneer School from 1792 to 1833 being added history on the Litchfield Female Academy kept by Miss Sarah Pierce and her nephew, John Pierce Brace* – compiled by the author. Cadmus Books, 1927.

W

Wadsworth Atheneum. *Bed Ruggs/ 1722-1833.* Introduction and Essay by William L. Warren. Hartford, Ct.: Wadsworth Atheneum, 1972.

Westall, Robert. *Antique Dust.* New York: Viking Penguin Books, 1989, England: Clio Press, 1990.

Williams, Ellen Louise Amidon. *In The Name of God, Amen Abstracts of Hyde County, North Carolina Wills Probated from 1709 through 1775.* Charlotte, N.C.: Herb Eaton Historical Publishers, 1989.

Winslow, Anna Green. *Diary of Anna Green Winslow – Boston School Girl 1771.* Alice Morse Earle, Editor. Boston: Houghton Mifflin Co., 1894.

Index

Firth, Daniel, 100
Fitch, Jedediah, 29
Flame stitch pattern, 10
Flock bed, 44
Florentine stitch, 10
Flournoy, Ann M., 47
Foote, Aaron, 28
Foote, Abigail, 26, 63
Foote, Anne (Clark), 26
Foote, Elizabeth, 26, 63
Foote, Elizabeth (Kimberly), 26, *pl.11, 12*
Foote, Esther, 26
Foote, Eunice, 26
Foote, Israel, 26
Foote, Mary, 26
Foote, Mary (Isham), 28
Foote, Nathaniel, 26, 28
Foote, Patience, 28, 51, *pl. 8, 9*
Foote, Patience (Skinner), 28
Foscue, Bell, 45
Foscue, Richard, 45
Foscue, Simon, 45
Fustic, 81

Gates, Caleb, 26
Geer family bed rug, 39
Gifford, Eliza, 39
Gifford, Gurdon, 39
Gillyflowers, 9
Glover, Mistress, 2
Glover, Rev. Jose, 5
Goau, Abraham, 44
Godey, L.A. & Co., 12
Goffe, John, 2
Governor Trumbull House, DAR, 25, 39, 78
Grant, Anne MacVicar, 16
Grant, Seth, 5
Green, Hannah (Carter), 29
Green, William, 29
Greenfield Village, Ford Museum, 51, 78
Gridley, Thomas, 13
Griswold, Joseph, 40

Guerrant, Esther, 46
Guerrant, Peter, 45, 90, 91
Gunby, Kirk, 95-97

Hale, David, 54
Hale, Elizabeth, 24
Hale, Elizabeth (Strong), 24
Hale, Enoch, 24
Hale, John, 24
Hale, Joseph, 24
Hale, Melissa, 25, 49
Hale, Nathan, 14, 24, 49, 54, 56
Hale, Nathan, (editor), 24
Hale, Octavia (Throop), 24
Hale, Polly, 24
Hale, Rebecca, 24
Hale, Rebekah (Harris), 23, 24, *pl.10*
Hale, Deacon Richard, 24
Hale, Richard, Jr., 54
Hale, Sally, 24
Hall, Aquila, 46
Hall, Aquila (Sr.), 46
Hall, John, 46
Harris, Judge Joseph, 24
Harris, Rebekah, 23, 24
Harvey, Abarilla, 46
Harvey, Margaret, 46
Harvey, Rachel, 46
Hill, George, 45
Hill, Mary, 45
Hill, Rachel, 45
Hinche, Elizabeth, 17
Historic Deerfield, 27, 42, 78, *pl. 5*
Holmes, Joseph, 98, 99
Honeysuckle, 9
Howard, Elizabeth, 34
Howard, Esther (Lyman), 34, 60, *pl. 4*
Howard, Nathaniel, 34
Howard, Stephen, 34
Howland, Elizabeth (Tilley), 85, 86
Hubbard, Daniel, 5
Huddle, Joseph, 47
Huntington, Rev. David, 26
Hyde, Asaph, 40
Hyde, Elihu, 40